"I can't say what I like most about this book. It could be the comprehensive range of recipes, from sausage rolls to stir fries and whole roast pig. Or it could be the tips that Michael has garnered from his 30+ years in the kitchen. But I think it might be Michael's voice—the way he writes like he's talking to you. He's the guide at the home cook's shoulder, the friend who likes to crack little jokes and share his contagious enthusiasm for getting people around the table."

ELIZABETH BAIRD

Over 100 delicious pork recipes for beginners and experts alike, to take you from breakfast to BBQ, and weeknight dinner to family feast.

After 30 years as a professional chef, Michael Olson knows how to get the most out of his food. These days, he's also a teacher and dinner-maker-in-chief, so he understands what home cooks are looking for when it's time to eat.

In *Living High Off the Hog*, Michael shares his wealth of knowledge and over 100 of his favorite pork recipes. First, he gives you a rundown on everything you need to know about pork—how to buy, store, butcher and prep various cuts, along with special sections on deli meats, charcuterie and BBQ. From there, he shares his must-have pantry items and most-used cooking techniques to set you up for success as you work through four extensive recipe chapters: The Deli Counter, Ground and Diced, Chops and Steaks and Roasts and Big Cuts. With recipes like Bacon Okonomiyaki, Caramelized Chili Pork with Peanuts & Lime, Schnitzel and Crispy Pork Belly, you'll find a huge variety of tastes and textures to explore. For special occasions, you can dig deep into the low-and-slow world of BBQ and experiment with one of his recipes for ribs, learn a new skill with a porchetta roast, or go hog wild and try your hand at roasting a whole pig.

With Michael's expert guidance, sense of humor and warm encouragement, you'll find recipes and learn techniques to cook familiar classics, as well as expand beyond your regular repertoire with exciting new ideas for all cuts of pork.

Whether he's cooking a laid-back meal with his wife, fellow chef Anna Olson, or entertaining a large group, Michael's main goal is to create simple yet delicious dishes from scratch, and enjoy them with those he loves. For Michael, that's what "living high off the hog" is—the good life of combining good food and great company around your table.

LIVING HIGH OFF THE HOG

Over 100 Recipes and Techniques to Cook Pork Perfectly

CHEF MICHAEL OLSON

appetite
by RANDOM HOUSE

Jaxali

Appetite by Random House™ and colophon are
registered trademarks of Penguin Random House LLC.

Library and Archives Canada Cataloguing in Publication
is available upon request.

ISBN: 978-0-14-753116-2
eBook ISBN: 978-0-14-753117-9

Cover and book design by Jennifer Griffiths
Photography by Janis Nicolay
Prop styling by Catherine Therrien
Illustrations by Gary Taxali
Illustrations on contents page are details from: Varken by Julie de Graag;
De Vliegende Actionist op de Waereld by Cornelis Anthonisz;
Vignet met een wapen met daarop een varken by Isaac Weissenbruch;
Schetsblad met studies van koeien by Gerard Bilders;
Studieblad met varkens by Willem Witsen/Rijksmuseum

Printed and bound in China

Published in Canada by Appetite by Random House™,
a division of Penguin Random House LLC.

www.penguinrandomhouse.ca

10 9 8 7 6 5 4 3 2 1

appetite
by RANDOM HOUSE

Penguin
Random House
Canada

OLSON HARDWARE

MODEL: #12 Computing Scale **MANUFACTURER**: IBM **YEAR**: 1919

NOTES: IBM started in the U.S. but set up shop in Toronto
in 1917. Back then, they made weigh scales, slicers and
tabulating machines.

Thank you to Anna for being the smartest, strongest, most talented, kindest and most honest person I could ever hope to meet. And you're beautiful!

Contents

THE DELI
COUNTER

PAGE 31

GROUND
AND DICED

PAGE 81

CHOPS
AND STEAKS

PAGE 161

ROASTS
AND BIG CUTS

PAGE 215

Introduction

"A LOOK THROUGH THE BUTCHER SHOP WINDOW"

If you have ever found yourself staring at the landscape of pork cuts in the cooler at the grocery store and felt lost as to what to buy (let alone how to cook and serve it), I am here to guide you. This book is packed with delicious pork recipes of all sorts—quick weekday suppers, appetizers for a few or many, elegant main courses and some BBQ and grilling fun. My goal is to help you expand the types of pork you purchase and then develop your confidence to transform those cuts into meals you'll be proud to share with family and friends.

And who am I to guide you on this journey? Well, I've been cooking pork for over 30 years—my entire professional career as a chef. I can offer the perspective of someone who has spent three decades in professional kitchens, planning menus, buying on a large scale, trimming, portioning, turning wholesale cuts into attractive single servings, and more. I've always loved working in kitchens, experiencing the adrenaline rush, the teamwork and the satisfaction of service. But, these days, having left the pro kitchen behind, I also understand what home cooks are looking for. I now focus on the practical angle of creating delicious meals in a timely manner without going overboard or getting too complicated.

Of course, cooking at home is entirely different from doing so professionally. There isn't the same urgency, budget or labor cost concern, and you get to eat the food! That said, regardless of the environment, I see cooking as a fun activity, almost like a puzzle to solve. Whether it's a meal for a holiday, a special occasion, or a regular Tuesday evening, I love the planning and shopping; choosing the right music; pulling out tablecloths, platters and glasses; and even buying fresh flowers. I experience an unbridled sense of joy as I bring it all together, checking off the to-dos from my list, grooving to the music and tasting great results as I wait for the guests to show.

But the best part of cooking is the sharing. Most of my meals are enjoyed with just my sweetie, Anna, and when I get the nod of approval from her, it's the best compliment ever. We're so well-suited and nerdily enthusiastic about food that we often plan our next meal while eating the one at hand. Anna, as many of you may know from her TV work, is a trained pastry chef. My culinary background is as a saucier (someone who cooks meat and prepares sauces). When we cook together, magic happens. We instinctively go to our own areas: Anna works on dessert and the vegetable sides, and I do the trimming, cook the meat and make the sauce. We clean as we go and laugh the whole time. Even if there are serious things to discuss, we do so in the kitchen. Now that my daughter, Mika, has become an accomplished cook in her own right, she gets in on the action. She grew up surrounded by good food and has always understood how to survive without having to order out. As a family, we hit our stride in the kitchen or at the table—and I'm good with that.

"Living high off the hog" is an old term used to suggest you're living the good life, able to eat the more expensive cuts of meat. In general, regardless of the animal, cuts from the upper (or "higher") part of the body are more tender than the lower ones—historically, only the poorest people would eat the jowls, belly, hock or feet. However, pork is an affordable meat choice for many, so in this case, the phrase is not about living beyond your means but rather about getting the most out of life by enjoying good food.

Pork is ubiquitous in North American cooking, and its versatility adapts well to global culinary flavor influences. A variety of cuts is available anywhere meat is sold, and we have a fresh, abundant, safe supply, thanks to the dedication of committed producers. Because pork is on the tables of many families at least once a week, home cooks need new ideas to build great meals and keep things fresh and interesting for both the cook and the family.

But, as common as pork is, we tend to buy the same few cuts we are familiar with. For you, that might be tenderloin and back ribs; for others, it could be loin chops and ground. With this collection of recipes and guiding tips, I want to broaden your hog horizons and help you try something new. In this book, I present my recipes in four chapters, comprising the major groups of cuts you will find at the grocery or butcher shop:

1. The Deli Counter (bacon, sausage, ham, etc.)

2. Ground and Diced

3. Chops and Steaks

4. Roasts and Big Cuts

This is not a BBQ book. While there are grilling recipes, this is about making great food with all the cuts available in the cooler and not being limited to a single cooking method. It's also not a "nose to tail" cookbook. Yes, we'll go beyond the cuts you normally buy, but you won't be eating snouts and ears. I will suggest buying tips, basic techniques and recommendations for side dishes. Covering a range of recipes, from simple everyday dishes to special occasion meals for a crowd, I hope to be the teachable voice that speaks to you about practical, delicious home cooking. Call me a bon vivant—I love the pleasures of the table. I believe good things come from the satisfaction of making something from scratch and especially from the feeling of accomplishment when people like the food you have made. It's not about ego. It's about communicating, nurturing and looking after your loved ones. I wrote this book because I'm really good at cooking pork, I'm willing to share and I love telling stories. I hope you enjoy cooking from it as much as I've enjoyed writing it!

Michael Olson

Meat in Society

There is no question that we live in a time when food is abundant and the consumption of meat protein is at an all-time high. Just over a century ago, people would have been shocked to walk through a supermarket and see the variety of food on offer. In fact, they would recognize very little on the shelves, as their understanding of food would be limited to those items available within a short distance of where they resided. Read any historical work on food, and it becomes easy to understand that the idea of having a roast chicken or steak on the table was indeed a sign of celebration or wealth. Our forebears would have included meat-based protein in meals when possible, but that would likely have been a small portion of salted, dried or smoked pork—the portion size would have been one that was economically and financially viable but also didn't require refrigeration.

It really wasn't that long ago that electricity and transportation radically changed how we eat. My father used to kid me about how he was lucky to get an orange for Christmas, and of course, I thought he was just taking a shot at me for how many gifts I hoped to get. I later realized he wasn't joking—his childhood took place during a time when it actually was a big deal to ship fresh fruit all the way from Florida to the frozen fields of the Canadian Prairies.

When you think about how food production has changed over the past 100 years, the shift from manual labor to automation and the development of electricity have caused a dramatic increase in our food output and availability. Producers were able to extend the day by lighting and heating their barns. Refrigeration changed how perishable foods were cooled, stored, shipped and displayed for sale. Instead of a family depending on an autumn pig slaughter to prepare bacon, ham, salami and other fare to last through cold weather, they could simply buy it as they needed it or store fresh meat in the freezer. Yet many kept on with old traditions, not only as a means of preserving the food and preventing spoilage but also because they loved the taste.

Smoking, fermenting and drying are no longer simply preventive measures but are cherished for the specific flavors and textures they bring to the table. I think the smoky aroma of bacon cooking in a pan wakes up a distant primal memory of being near home, a safe, warm place with good food. Many of my Italian-Canadian friends make a type of salami called soppressata that takes three months to cure. They don't do it to save money—they do it to spend time with their families. I recall one friend telling me of the heartache of sitting with his mother and sister, eating the last soppressata his father had made with them before he passed away. They sat around the kitchen table, cutting thin slices to savor, with tears streaming down their cheeks. These shared moments with family and friends make us who we are, and meat has always been a part of that.

Buying Pork

DELI MEATS

Pork can be found in just about every grocery store or butcher shop in both processed and fresh form. Processed pork has been cured or cooked to make it last longer and lend a specific taste or texture. This includes bacon, wieners, ham, pâté, salami, smoked sausage, dried ham (such as prosciutto) and much more. Processed pork almost always has nitrates added to it as a preservative. The nitrates prevent food spoilage by warding off bacteria growth and also keeps the meat a distinct pink color (you will recognize this color in sliced cold cuts). Although it is suggested that we avoid eating too much food with nitrates and nitrites, the reality is that these preservatives prevent people from getting sick.

FRESH MEATS

Supermarkets will have a range of fresh cuts, either refrigerated or frozen, and sometimes marinated, but if I want a specific cut or trim, I go to a butcher shop. Most supermarkets do not typically cut the meat on-site, as they do not have trained butchers on staff. When I buy fresh pork, I plan on using it within a few days. There is not a generally accepted benefit to aging fresh pork the way people do with beef. I use ground pork the same day I buy it and keep roasts and chops for 3 or 4 days.

FROZEN MEATS

The best way to thaw frozen pork is in the fridge overnight or through the day. You can speed up the defrost time of vacuum-packed pork by setting it in trickling cold water, but I avoid leaving it on the counter at room temperature. It's really not food-safe in the long run. The problem with thawing at room temperature is that the center of the meat could be frozen solid but the outside could be thawed and likely getting warmer than recommended. I will freeze meat that has been cooked but won't refreeze raw meat that was previously frozen. Pork will keep for up to 6 months if frozen in airtight packaging, but the fat can start to degrade after this time.

Hommer Van der Meer

The Basics of Butchering

When an animal comes out of the slaughter, it is divided into wholesale cuts that are turned into portions and roasts that are ready to cook (also known as fabrication). The four main wholesale cuts from a side of pork are:

1. Shoulder
2. Loin
3. Belly
4. Leg

Each piece is relatively the same weight, roughly 20% of the weight of the whole dressed side ("dressed" means the head and internal organs have been removed). The remaining 20% of the animal (the head, tail and organ meats) is also used but is not normally seen at meat counters. Chefs will buy wholesale cuts and cut them into smaller portions for cooking but also use all the trim (for sausage) and bones (for stock or sauce). Most of the pork home cooks purchase is in fabricated portions, but you can buy large roasts like whole butts (shoulder), loin or legs.

GRADING

One thing about buying pork compared to beef is that pork does not carry a designation on the grade. Grading is actually a complicated process that most people do not understand, but it does help explain something about buying pork. First of all, any meat that is commercially available in Canada or the United States is inspected by a trained person to make sure it is safe to eat. In the case of beef, the processor then has the option for the inspector to grade the meat by measuring muscle size and the amount of intramuscular fat (or marbling). The result will depend on the breed of the animal and the feeding practices used. Now, this is where it gets interesting: there are many varieties of milk- and meat-producing cattle, so the variation among breeds is great. These differences have to do with the size of the muscles and how the muscles are distributed over the carcass. Grading allows the customer to know ahead of time what the expectation of tenderness should be. However, the consistency of pork makes this step less of a factor (the gene pool is much smaller), and after working with so many loins, tenderloins, shoulders and other cuts over the years, I can vouch for the fact that they are pretty much the same every time. This is a good thing.

HERITAGE BREEDS

Most of the pork in North America is produced from Yorkshire, Landrace, Duroc, Berkshire and Hampshire breeds (these are very recognizable pigs) and is familiar at the grocery meat counter: pink with a fairly small amount of white fat. Chefs are also highly interested in exploring the heritage breeds of pork, such as Tamworth or Mangalitsa, which may have been common on farms a few generations back but have been pushed aside for not being practical or popular. This pork tends to appear on adventurous restaurant menus or in a few small butcher shops. Chefs love these breeds for making charcuterie because of their intense flavor and high amount of fat. For the most part, they are not seen in regular circles, simply because there aren't that many of these pigs in production. As a result, I don't have specific recipes using Tamworth or Mangalitsa pork (these do not look like regular pigs—in fact, the Mangalitsa has a curly fur coat), but I encourage you to try them when you find them on a menu.

FRESH CUTS

Now that you've learned about how the pork has gotten to your butcher's counter, here is some helpful information on the meat itself.

SHOULDER: This muscle group has slightly darker flesh than the lean loin cuts (muscle that does more "work" is always darker from increased blood flow). The high fat–to–lean meat ratio (about 20% fat) is ideal for making sausage and keeps the meat moist while cooking. The 20% fat also gives a juicy finish to roasts cut from the shoulder. The wholesale cut is called a New York shoulder and is divided into two parts: the butt and picnic.

1 The butt is the upper half of the shoulder (the shoulder blade), nearest the head, and can be purchased whole (for pulled pork), with or without bones, cut into smaller roasts or chops, diced for braising and minced for ground pork. Part of the butt is the capicola muscle (my favorite for BBQ), which can be bought whole or cut into capicola steaks.

2 The picnic is the lower part of the shoulder, nearest the front foot of the pig. Picnic can be purchased as a fresh roast, with or without bones, but also appears as a whole ham in the deli counter. The whole picnic with skin on makes a wonderful slow roast—the skin gets crisp, and the meat falls apart as if it were braised (see Roast Picnic Shoulder with Apple Onion Gravy, page 251).

LOIN: This is the part of the animal that's most common and is easily identified (like pork chops). The loin section is the top muscle that runs along the backbone. It includes back ribs and the tenderloin muscle. You can find whole

or half boneless loins in supermarkets if you want to cut your own roasts and steaks. Butcher shops will cut the loin into chops from end to end, to make up mixed packages, or sell them according to section—the loin can be divided into three sections, each with many possible cuts.

1 The rib end section is the equivalent of the prime rib roast on beef. It can be purchased as a rib roast, trimmed to make a rack (one of my favorites), cut into rib chops or boneless rib steaks, split through the rib bones to make country-style ribs or made into back ribs. The portion of the rib bone nearest the spine is the back rib, and it has the lean and meaty loin muscle running next to it. The rib meat between the bones is not as tender as the loin, but is very flavorful and tender when properly cooked. Back rib bones tend to have a higher proportion of meat to bone when compared to side ribs. These are also called "baby back ribs" and are more expensive than side ribs. There are usually a dozen ribs on a rack, and each rack will weigh around 2¼ lb (1 kg). I always buy too much (I'm an enthusiastic cook), but you can usually get away with one rack for every two or three people.

2 The center cut is the lean muscle that's used for boneless center roast, loin steaks, loin chops, fast-fry chops and butterflied loin steak. These are easy to stuff, cook and carve but can be dry if overcooked. The boneless loin can be cut into portions and pounded to make cutlets or schnitzel.

3 The sirloin end is the part of the loin section nearest to the back leg. This is also where the tenderloin rests, under the backbone. Sirloin roast, sirloin (T-bone) chops and boneless sirloin steaks are all found here. Meat from this area is darker than the center cuts of the loin and stays moist during cooking.

TENDERLOIN: The tenderloin comes from the rear part of the loin section and is one of the most popular quick-cooking pork cuts. Each weighs around 1 lb (450 g) and can be left whole or cut into little medallions or strips. There is a small section of "silver skin" that can be removed to make the meat tender and able to absorb marinade quickly. The tenderloin is ideal for dinner for two and can be trimmed, portioned and cooked in less than 30 minutes.

BELLY: The belly gives up two of the most recognizable parts of the pork world: ribs and bacon. The majority of bellies are usually further processed for bacon, but more and more often, I see fresh belly in stores. I never ate belly except in the form of bacon when I was growing up, but now I roast it as a treat.

1 Side ribs are the lower portion of bones that run along the belly. The wholesale belly cut has the side ribs attached, and these are removed when making belly (this must be where the term "spare rib" comes from). Side ribs have a slightly lower meat-to-bone ratio, and the bone itself is somewhat flat in shape. The less tender belly meat runs along this part of the rack, so the meat in between each bone is not as tender as it is in the back rib. A full rack of side ribs is less uniform than back ribs, as it comes with a cartilage breastbone and tapers off to small ribs that move toward the back end of the rib cage. Butchers can fix this by making the side ribs into the St. Louis cut, whereby the breastbone and tail portion are removed to square up the meat. These are the ribs you find at rib fests, and they are the choice of most serious BBQ ribbers. They're less expensive than back ribs and very tasty. Like back ribs, St. Louis rib racks weigh around 2 lb (1 kg).

2 Side pork can be purchased sliced (see Grilled Korean Style Belly, page 191) or in 2 lb (1 kg) blocks (see Crispy Pork Belly, page 229). It can be grilled, braised or roasted, and although it's quite fatty, it has a wonderful, rich meaty taste. This recognizable cut is often seen as bacon.

LEG: This is most recognizable as a whole ham. The leg has three muscles (the inside, outside and tip) that can be turned into roasts and steaks, diced for sautéing or even turned into cutlets. The meat is pale pink, quite lean and not as tender as the loin. If you see a pork roast sold in netting, it is likely from this part of the animal. We use the leg at my school to show the student chefs how to butcher—from these parts, they make roasts, cutlets for sandwiches, kebabs and ground pork for meat pie.

The other part of the leg that's sold fresh is the hock, which is less tender, so it must be slowly braised rather than cooked using a dry heat method (like grilling). When done properly, the meat will be soft, tender and full of flavor. A great example is Oompahpah Schweinehaxe: Crispy Pork Hocks (page 274).

PORK CUTS

shoulder blade   butt chops
   roast   diced
picnic   ground
butt   sausage
capicola   hock

rack   back ribs
rib chops   tenderloin
fast fry   cutlets
t-bone   loin steaks
center chop   + Country
peameal bacon   Style Ribs

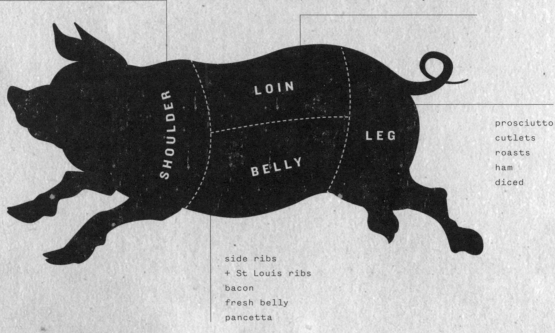

LOIN

SHOULDER

BELLY

LEG

prosciutto
cutlets
roasts
ham
diced

side ribs
+ St Louis ribs
bacon
fresh belly
pancetta

SHOULDER

Shoulder, blade (butt), boneless

Shoulder, blade (butt), capicola, boneless

Shoulder, picnic, hock-on

Shoulder blade roast

Shoulder blade, capicola steak, boneless

Belly, side
pork roast

Belly, side pork

Belly, side ribs

Loin, boneless

Tenderloin

Rib roast, boneless

Rib roast, rack

Pork T-bone

Loin center chop,
boneless

Rib chop

Loin chop, frenched

Rib chop, boneless

Loin, back ribs

Leg inside
scaloppini,
boneless

Charcuterie

Charcuterie is the domain of butchers and cooks who prepare meat by curing or cooking it to a state of being ready to eat. It has a long history and was originally used to preserve meat before we had electric refrigeration. Our ancestors figured out that meat would not spoil if it was "cured" by being salted and dried, fermented or cooked. Before they even knew what bacteria was, they determined that there were a number of ways to remove the conditions that promoted food spoilage. I've outlined several methods below.

CURING

Curing is done by salting the meat to remove water. The less water there is in a food, the longer it will last at room temperature. Consider a sun-dried tomato: it can sit on the counter for months, and nothing much will happen to it, but a fresh tomato will completely rot and turn into a pile of goo in the same time. This is the way that ham like prosciutto is made: fresh pork legs are salted to remove the excess water and then hung to air-dry at a controlled pace. It just happens that the area most famous for these hams—Parma, Italy—also has the best natural conditions of humidity and air movement for slow, steady drying. After a lengthy rest of up to 2 years, the ham can be sliced thinly and stored without a problem. Outside Italy, Spain boasts its *jamon serrano* (mountain ham) and *iberico* (from a specific breed of pig that forages for acorns), and these hams are salted and dried in a way similar to their Italian cousins. And the method is not limited to Europe: China has a salted, dried version called *jinhua* ham. In addition to pork legs, the same salting and drying

can be applied to loin, capicola, jowl or belly to produce amazing cold cuts. Some of the most famous pasta dishes from Italy use cured jowl (see Fettuccine all'Amatriciana, page 77) or belly (see Spaghetti Carbonara, page 74).

FERMENTING

Fermented sausage, like salami, has a low pH, making it slightly acidic, which prevents spoilage. Fermenting is the same process used to make bread or wine: yeast eats natural sugars and produces carbon dioxide (which makes bread rise) and alcohol (hello, wine). A second natural fermentation can occur when good bacteria eat the alcohol and produce vinegar or acetic acid. This is what happens to cabbage to turn it into sauerkraut, and to salted cucumbers to make sour pickles. In the case of salami, meat is ground and seasoned, and a yeast starter is added. It is put into casings, just like fresh sausage, but then allowed to dry. The yeast starts the fermentation. When the alcohol turns to vinegar, it changes the pH in the salami, making bacterial growth impossible. It is counterintuitive to consider leaving raw ground meat to ferment, but it ends up producing a food-safe product with a lengthy shelf life. Think about it—you have kept salami in your fridge for a really long time, haven't you?

SMOKING

Smoking is an especially interesting form in the charcuterie playbook. It's likely that, after realizing salt helped make meat last longer, people then stored the meat somewhere close by, away from pests, like in the chimney area near the wood fire used for cooking. This would help dry the meat, and of course, the meat picked up a smoky flavor and, to a degree, tannins from the wood that act as a preservative. The smoky aroma and flavor is very agreeable, and this practice became its own curing method. Different geographical areas would use specific woods for smoke and lend their own distinct regional flair. The original Black Forest ham, now common just about anywhere, would have started in Germany's south, using a specific recipe, timeline, wood and storage. The Europeans have been protective of their naming processes and origins; this extends beyond meat to products like cheese and wine. In Italy, the rules for producing Parma ham would make your head spin—from the type of pig to what it eats, its size and age, the curing salt used, the timing and so on.

Bacon is one of the most popular forms of pork in North America. Bellies are cured and hot-smoked to partial doneness, and then we cook slices at home to a crisp state. The aroma of bacon is a magical thing for many (yeah, I'm looking at you), and bacon has become a crutch for many other foods. When crisped and chopped, it becomes a vital part of salad toppings and entices many to eat vegetables they otherwise might not try. It is also used to lend moisture and smoky, salty character when wrapped around lean cuts or to hold together meatloaf (see Bacon Wrapped Meatloaf with Orange Marmalade & Beer Glaze, page 146).

A whole roster of other smoked foods fills the deli case, including garlic kielbasa, Hungarian smoked sausage, wieners, smoked ribs and ham hocks.

COOKING

Cooking extends the life of fresh meat by removing water and ridding the surface of any trace of bacteria. Cooked pâté, terrines, meat pies, hams, and roast or smoked meats will last much longer than raw. Our beloved holiday ham is first cured and then smoked and, finally, cooked to the right temperature (see Ham Waldorf Salad, page 45, and Ham & Barley Soup, page 61).

Mike and Valerio, the Sorrenti Brothers

BBQ

A true celebration of all things pork can never stray too far from delicious BBQ. What is it that makes it so appealing to so many? Is it the warm, fuzzy feeling it produces, the aroma of the wood fire, the soft, juicy texture of the meat or the sweet, salty spice of the dark brown "bark" on the outside? Or maybe it's the fact that you can't rush it—you have to relax and appreciate the downtime it takes to get to the point of "tender-ridiculiciousness" over low temperatures? Whatever the answer is for you, BBQ is a great democratizer, loved by bricklayers and brain surgeons, young and old, whoever you are.

The difference between grilling and BBQ is a big deal. Grilling is cooking single portions on a hot grill with the lid open. This is what most people do with steaks and chops on a gas grill. It's a perfectly fine cooking method and does not take much time.

On the other hand, when you use BBQ as a verb, it refers to the process of cooking larger pieces of meat for a long time over low temperatures in the presence of smoke. There are regional variations in the United States, but generally, there is a "rub" of salt, sugar and spice on the outside of the meat and, most often, a sweet, sticky glaze that is applied for the last part of cooking. BBQ in this sense does not have grill marks on it but rather an even color, often dark and shiny when glazed. The benchmarks of the BBQ world are ribs and pulled pork, made from the butt portion of the shoulder. Ribs are sliced into individual bones, and pulled pork is cooked to such a tender state that it does not slice but rather falls apart—"pulling" refers to the action of shredding and breaking the meat into chunks using two dinner forks. The low-and-slow BBQ

method is based on the food of the American South from generations back, deeply influenced by African-American cooks who smoke-roasted large cuts or whole carcasses of pork over indirect heat from a wood fire at a low temperature. In Texas, beef is cooked BBQ style, but across the eastern United States, it is all pork. Over the past couple of decades, Canada has embraced the American style of BBQ, and it is popular in restaurants, at festivals and, most importantly, in backyards from coast to coast to coast.

RIBS

Ribs are a BBQ standard, and once you get the hang of cooking them, they're an easy meal that will please your family and friends. There are so many recipes and methods that it can be confusing, and attitudes have changed toward basic preparation. Those in the BBQ world, the ones who dedicate time to competing in BBQ contests and festivals, are absolutely against the concept of boiling ribs. Yet this was common practice just one generation ago. The method suggested cooking the ribs in a flavorful liquid to make them tender and then finishing them off on a hot grill with a glaze of BBQ sauce.

These days, you'll see professional BBQ chefs using a dry heat method, which is the best in my opinion, too. It may take a little longer, but it doesn't require two cooking techniques, forcing you to clean up twice, plus you won't be pouring what ends up being a BBQ pork stock down the drain after boiling. Lastly, this method tenderizes the "finger meat," which is the muscle between the rib bones that technically would benefit from braising or another moist form of cooking. But the low-and-slow method is nearly like braising, as it is done in a closed environment because the BBQ lid is down.

BUTT

As I've mentioned, pork butt is the upper part of the shoulder, not the rear end. "Butt" was a term used in the old days to refer to a barrel used for shipping and storing everything from crackers to nails. Pork shoulders were salted and packed into barrels for shipping, and somehow the name stuck.

Butt is the best choice for feeding a crowd when it comes to BBQ, because one piece, made into pulled pork, will feed a dozen or more people. But if I am not cooking for a crowd, I will ask the butcher for a fresh capicola. This is part of the butt, a cylinder shape with a diameter about the size of a large grapefruit. Any butcher shop that makes sausage will have these in the back, and you can order them ahead of time.

The key to producing flavor in pulled pork is the development of the bark, which is the dark crust on the exterior with all the spices and salt, where the sugar in the rub caramelizes. As this bark is shredded and worked into the meat, the

meat picks up the sweet, salty character and smoky aroma. A handful of pulled pork fresh off the grill, stuffed into a bun with coleslaw, is a beautiful treat indeed.

EQUIPMENT FOR BBQ

You can make delicious BBQ-style meats in the oven (see Honey Garlic Oven Roasted Back Ribs with Sesame Crunch, page 271), but for the best results, you should go outside.

GAS GRILL: BBQ can be made on a gas grill by using the indirect heat method, which means turning on a burner and cooking the meat on the other side of the grill, away from the heat source (you can add wood chips for smoke). But when I want to really do it right, I cook over a wood fire—this is why I prefer either a charcoal-burning ceramic egg (like the Big Green Egg) or a pellet grill (I have a Traeger).

CHARCOAL: I really like the aroma of burning charcoal. There is something absolutely primal about lighting and looking after a fire to feed "your people." This style of grill depends on airflow to control the temperature, and I see it as more of a charcoal-fired oven than an open grill. Keeping the lid down is great for containing the smoky aromas in low-and-slow cooking, but also excellent for grilling at high temperatures. You start the fire and then adjust the vents, thereby controlling the air intake (fuel) and exhaust (the draw or flow). Low temperatures can be held by restricting the air flow through the vents; opening up the vents will put the grill at super-heat range for quick searing. It takes a bit of time to get used to this technique, but it's a great all-purpose method for smoking, grilling and low-and-slow BBQ.

PELLET GRILL: I have to admit I've really enjoyed the convenience of the pellet-style grill. Here's how it works: Compressed hardwood pellets are stored in a hopper and fed by an auger (a sort of corkscrew that moves the pellets as it turns) to an electric firebox burner so that the burning pellets are the source of

both heat and smoke. The speed of the auger is controlled by a thermostat, so it is as easy as loading in the meat and following the old "set it and forget it" method, to coin a phrase. I BBQ so often at home that it is nearly automatic. I know ribs will take about 4 hours and a shoulder cut between 8 and 10 hours, so I simply plan the day around it. If dinner is at seven and we're having ribs, they go in the smoker at three, giving me plenty of time to continue on with the day and get the rest of the meal ready.

SMALL TOOLS: In addition to your grill(s), you would do well to have a set of tools for when you want to get your BBQ on. I'm a firm believer in having the right tools for the job, and there are plenty of choices for grilling accessories on the market—here are some I recommend.

- **Instant thermometer** (see page 17).

- **Digital thermometer** (see on page 17).

- **Tongs.** I always have several pairs of outdoor tongs. One set is for handling raw meat, and the other is for cooked meat, to avoid cross contamination.

- **Fork.** I use a long carving fork to turn, lift and carve large cuts of meat that are too heavy or big for tongs.

- **Basting brush.** Choose a dishwasher-friendly silicone one instead of natural fiber bristles. It's used for coating the meat with mustard or glazing it with sauce.

- **Grill cleaner.** I have gotten away from using wire brushes for cleaning the grill, as there is always a chance that a stray piece of wire can get into the food. Instead, I opt for a wooden paddle spoon with a handful of scrunched-up foil to use as a brush. It works so well!

- **Lighter.** To light charcoal, I avoid using chemical lighting fluid or paraffin starter cubes. I like the hot-air electric charcoal starter made by Looftlighter or Kamado Joe. The starter is like a paint-remover gun and gets the charcoal fired up in no time. I also have a backup electric "horseshoe" lighter.

- **Spray bottle.** I keep a food-grade plastic spray bottle for finely glazing marinades directly onto the food while cooking.

- **Chip box.** If you want to add smoke when using a grill, chip boxes can be filled with wood chips for that extra flavor.

- **Metal ash can.** If you use a charcoal grill, you will have to empty out ashes, and it's best to do so into a can that won't melt if the ashes are hot.

The Prep Shift: Kitchen Basics

THE TOOLS IN MY KITCHEN

Before you start to cook, you need the proper tools for the job.

Knives

Knives are the most important kitchen tool (after your hands) and are a highly personal choice, as they must fit your hand as comfortably as a pair of shoes fits your feet. When I started cooking, professional knives were only found in specialty stores, but now well-known brands are available everywhere. Older-style knives are made of high-carbon steel and hold their edge well, but they can rust and will need a lot of pampering and care. Most knives on the market these days are made with stainless steel blades. The better quality ones cost a small fortune, but they will last a lifetime. There are so many shapes and varieties out there that it's tough to say which is best. My advice is to simply shop around and hold them in your hand before deciding. You only need a small set, so don't feel like you have to buy the whole kit to start.

FRENCH: Also known as a chef's knife, this is your basic blade for chopping, dicing and slicing. If I could have only one type of knife, this would be it. Blade lengths vary, so choose the right size for everyday comfort. For example, my wife and I have some knives that we share and others that suit us better individually (I have large hands; she does not). My favorite brands are Mac, Ivo, Global and Victorinox. Artisan knife making has become a big deal lately, and many chefs have custom-made knives with specialty wood handles, Japanese steel and other attributes to make them special. Don't sweat it, though—you can get by just fine with a regular knife.

PARING: A short, simple knife, it's used for peeling onions and shallots, trimming fruits and even peeling coarse vegetables. I have a good one but usually reach for one of the half-dozen cheapies that go in the dishwasher and can be used for opening bags, cutting strawberries and just about any job that requires a sharp edge. These can be purchased at a supermarket and will last 6 months to 1 year. Unlike a French knife, which always makes contact with food while on a cutting board, paring knives are best used while the food is held in your hand.

BONING: Also called a filleting knife, this one has a sharp point for trimming and shaping meats and removing bones. There are both flexible and stiff blade varieties, each with benefits in a butcher shop (flexible ones are perfect for delicate bone removal). If you don't have one of these, a sharp paring knife will do in most cases.

SLICING: This knife has a long, thin blade and is used for carving meats. It is ideal for ham and large roasts, as a whole slice can be carved with one pass of the blade. Slicing knives are not used every time you cook, so they're not essential if you have a good-sized French knife.

BREAD: This serrated knife has scalloped edges that allow you to saw through the crispy crust of bread and items cooked in pastry. These do not get sharpened on a stone but will keep their edge pretty much forever.

Cutting Boards

Even if you have wooden surfaces in your kitchen, it's advisable to use a cutting board to protect your counter and make cleanup easier, especially when using raw meats. I always have five or six—small and large, wooden and plastic—on the go. I hand-wash wood ones, and the plastic boards go in the dishwasher. I also have some that are very handsome, so I use them as serving platters and for meat and cheese trays. I like to use wood (such as bamboo) for vegetables and cooked meats, and plastic for raw meats. To avoid having the cutting board slip or move when being used, I cut small sheets of vinyl drawer liner to put underneath to anchor the board in place. You can also use a damp paper towel.

Stainless Steel Bowls

I use these bowls every time I cook. They're great for handling ingredients, using as a temporary bin for food scraps, making dressings, marinating and many more tasks. I prefer stainless steel to glass or ceramic as it won't break or

Knife Tips:

1 Keep your knives clean and avoid banging them around in an open drawer. Rather, store them in a countertop knife block or in a way that does not dull the sharp edge.

2 Knives can be sharpened on occasion by a pro, or you can look into buying a sharpening stone if you're so inclined. Use a knife steel to maintain the edge on a regular basis—I do this every time I use the knife.

3 Good-quality knives should be washed by hand, not in the dishwasher. Never put a knife into a sink full of soapy water (someone might reach into the sink and cut themselves). After I'm done using a knife, I wash it, wipe it dry and put it away.

stain. These bowls are quick to clean, affordable and easy to store, because they nest together in a drawer. I don't use them for food storage, though, as a bag or square shape takes up less space in the fridge.

Measuring Devices

For these recipes, it's important to keep measuring cups, spoons and a digital scale close at hand. When I measure meat on the scale, I put down a piece of plastic wrap first to keep it clean.

Thermometers

There are three types of thermometers I use in the kitchen.

1 **Oven thermometer.** This one stays in the oven so I can see what the actual temperature is in there, not just what it says on the dial, which can often be incorrect.

2 **Probe thermometer.** I also count on an in-place probe thermometer that stays in the roast while cooking and displays the temperature on a small unit outside the oven. These are easy to read, can be set to a desired internal temperature and also have a built-in timer. They are inexpensive and easy to find. I have used one by Polder for over a decade.

3 **Instant-read thermometer.** This one works by sticking the probe into the densest part of the meat (not hitting the bone) to take a reading. It's then removed right away, unlike the in-place probe thermometer. These have slim probes so they don't leave a hole in single portions like steaks or chops. I use a pro tool called Thermapen. It can check roasts and individual chops, and go outside to the BBQ and likely has a few uses I haven't thought of yet. The accuracy and quality are excellent. It's not cheap, but one should last for a very long time, providing your nephew doesn't lay eyes on it!

Food Processor/Blender

There are many brands and sizes of food processors, and I don't have to tell you the various attributes of this tool—I use it for purees of all sorts, making bread crumbs, making Chimichurri (page 203) and pulsing meats to either a shred or to a fine paste (see Pork Rillettes, page 90, and Pojarski Chops with Mushroom Cream, page 197). The other option is an upright blender, which can do many of the same functions. I also keep an immersion blender nearby for pureeing soups right in the pot, and making salad dressings and herb purees.

Sieve

If you make your own stock, you'll have to strain it, and a decent strainer or sieve will catch all the particles in the liquid so you can remove them. The best sauces are strained before using to remove herb stems and any lumps.

Containers

Square or rectangular glass containers with plastic lids are effective for storing prep, marinades or leftovers. I also use a lot of resealable plastic bags for storing small amounts of the same. If I need to freeze something, I use a bag rather than a hard container. Foods kept in the fridge should be used within a few days, so I don't label and date them, but I try to do so for everything that goes into the freezer so it can be identified and the date checked.

Pots

Preparing soups and sauces, braising, boiling pasta, cooking vegetables, making rice or potatoes—the uses of pots are broad in everyday cooking, and you know it's a family gathering when you are using every pot and pan in the house. I like to have a variety of sizes for different tasks and would always recommend choosing ones that are well-made and have some heft, as a heavy, thick-bottomed pot is less likely to scorch food. I use an induction cooktop at home, so I don't have aluminum pots or pans (induction-friendly pots are easy to identify because a magnet will stick to the bottom). For everyday cooking of vegetables or boiling water for pasta, I use stainless steel pots. If I want to make a stew, soup or pot roast,

I prefer an enamel-covered iron pot with a lid. I have been a collector of Le Creuset pots for decades, both vintage and new, so there is no shortage at home. I think I have always had a soft spot for them, as my mother got a set as a wedding gift and some are still in use nearly 70 years later. If you do have enamel pots, don't use them if they are chipped inside, but retire them to a display shelf in your kitchen.

Pans and Skillets

I employ the same approach to pans as I do to pots—we have a whole range and use the ones best suited to the job. For most things, I first look to a good-quality nonstick frying pan and freely admit the biggest factor there is my laziness. It is easy to clean up, requires no scrubbing and takes less than 2 minutes to wash and dry. I also have stainless, cast iron and enamel-coated cast iron. The weight of a skillet has a bearing on how well it holds heat for searing to develop color. The heavier it is, the longer it will hold onto heat. If I am cooking thick pork chops and want to brown them to create a golden crust, I will use a cast iron skillet. And of course, good-looking skillets can double as serving dishes on a buffet or kitchen island. Even if I cook items in a different pan, I will reheat them for a dinner party in a large, colorful skillet and put it on a trivet right on the dinner table.

Baking Tools

My wife is a baker, so I have a couple of real advantages. First, she keeps a well-stocked baking equipment cupboard, but second, and more importantly, she helps if I need a dough or some advice. I often use her loaf tins, square cake tins, rolling pin and springform pans (see Pork-a-Leekie Pie, page 84). I also use her baking sheets, lined with parchment paper, for reheating dishes or melting cheese in the oven.

Roasting Pans

Sheet pans can be used for roasting stuffed chops or heating schnitzels, and I always like to use a rack set over a parchment-lined pan for better air circulation (Panko Crusted Tonkatsu, on page 163, benefits from this to get the top and bottom crispy). But higher-sided roasting pans are better for cooking a large roast to feed a group of people, as the heavy bottom holds the heat and you can use it to make the sauce after the roast is removed.

Meat Hammer

Whether you call it a tenderizer (sounds chemical), a meat hammer (sounds Viking) or a cutlet bat (you should have seen the look on my wife's face the first time I asked her to pass the cutlet bat—chiroptophobia = fear of bats), this is a tool used to flatten meat to a thin state. All-metal ones can go in the dishwasher, and wooden-handled models should be handwashed.

What Is the Deal with Well-Done Pork?

We tend to learn many things in our formative years that we never question or challenge, but accept because someone told us so. My mom always reminded me that pork had to be cooked well-done and told me to never eat raw bacon or I'd get worms. OK, that is a pretty good incentive not to question it further. I'd bet some of you have grown up with a similar story. There is some truth behind it, but let's take a look at where this comes from.

Many family farms would have had a variety of animals in circulation, in addition to grain, fruit and vegetable crops. Part of the standard practice for a small family farm in our recent past would have been to recycle leftovers from the kitchen into the daily food rations for the pigs. This would include not only vegetable peelings but also uneaten leftovers from the plates. Sadly, a human-borne parasite called trichinosis could easily be transmitted from the mouth of little Jimmy to Arnold the Pig and then eventually come back to the kitchen in the meat. To wipe out any chance of trichinosis, people would thoroughly cook the meat to the well-done stage, plus a little extra, just for safety. But the practice of table scraps going to feed the animals stopped a long time ago, and commercial production prohibits it, so Canada and the United States basically eradicated the problem over a generation ago.

And although we've vastly improved our food safety, the challenge that chefs and home cooks face when serving pork that isn't well-done gets a little more complicated when we compare the pork we eat today to what our grandparents ate. Through selective breeding, the pork we normally get at the store these days is leaner than what our relatives ate back in the day, so an old family recipe that calls for overcooking can lead to a dry texture in a lean cut. Old habits die hard. Even if you have scientific evidence proving it is all right to eat pink pork tenderloin, you will have a hard time convincing your aunt or granddad (or even yourself) that you are not out to cause harm.

In the United States, the USDA's current recommendation for cooking pork is for roasts and chops to reach an internal temperature of 145°F (63°C), with a 3-minute resting period; it's 160°F (71°C) for any ground meat, sausage or organ meats. The recommendation from Health Canada is to cook all pork to 160°F (71°C). I **tend to follow the USDA guidelines, and cook roasts and chops to 145°F (63°C), so that is what you can expect to see in the recipe methods throughout this book.** Regardless of which guideline you follow, the best way to eat safely is to use a good-quality digital thermometer to test the doneness. Be sure to put the probe into the middle of the roast, meatloaf or chop to get an accurate reading of the densest part of the meat. There are exceptions, of course, and this is where texture comes into play. For a braised dish or low-and-slow BBQ for pulled pork, you want to cook it to a point where it has a texture that falls apart. Shoulder has enough fat in it to stay juicy even when well-cooked. In fact, many BBQ aficionados take shoulder to the 185°F (85°C) mark. Personally, I tend to cook lean roasts, such as loin, a little less to avoid drying out, but I cook shoulder well-done for the fall-apart texture. Whatever you choose, do some research and make sure you feel comfortable with your decision.

SAFE FOOD HANDLING

Raw meat has to be handled carefully to ensure it is safe to eat. You can follow these simple tips, but always use common sense.

1   Refrigerate the meat as soon as you get home from the store. If you will not get home in a reasonable amount of time after shopping, take a cooler with ice to store the meat at a safe temperature (below 40°F/5°C).

2   Thaw meat in the fridge overnight, not on the counter.

3   Store meat on the bottom shelf of the fridge in a resealable plastic bag set on a tray, plate or bowl to prevent any blood from leaking. Never store raw meat on a shelf above cooked foods or any foods that will be served uncooked.

4   Wash your hands before and after handling meat.

5   Sanitize your cutting board after raw meat has been on it and before cutting foods on the board. If it's plastic, you can clean it in the dishwasher; if it's wood, wash with hot soapy water, rinse, use a kitchen sanitizer and air-dry.

6   Use a thermometer to check the internal temperature of meat as you are cooking it.

YES

Cooking Techniques

VEGETABLE PREP

The Three-Bowl System is a fundamental part of food preparation. It helps you work effectively and keep the prep area tidy. Use three bowls (or plates) for the following items.

- **Raw, unprepped product:** Your onions, carrots, herbs, etc., should be washed and placed in a dish for easy access. This will keep them contained.

- **Discarded scraps:** The second bowl is where you put the peels or trimmings, in order to keep your working area clean. The contents of the bowl will eventually go into the compost.

- **Finished product:** The third bowl will have cleaned, edible items that are either ready to cook (like green beans) or ready to be processed further (like carrots that are ready to be shaped).

PEELING: Use a vegetable peeler for removing the peel and ends of carrots, potatoes, parsnips, etc. A paring knife or the bowl of a spoon is more suitable for removing the skin of fresh ginger. Garlic heads can be separated into cloves by pressing firmly on the root end. Crack the cloves with a meat hammer or another flat surface and remove the paper. Shallots and onions should have their skin taken off with a paring knife, but make sure to leave a part of the root end attached to hold the onion together while it is being diced.

PICKING HERBS: Herbs should be washed in cold water and then picked off the stem. Some stems are edible (like cilantro), while others are tough (like thyme) but can go into a stock or soup for flavor. Unused fresh herbs can be stored in the fridge in a plastic bag or upright in a container of water covered with a damp paper towel.

MEAT PREP

Trimming Silver Skin

Most pork is quite lean, so you won't have to remove much fat, but I always check and trim any dark blood spots or bits of tough cartilage or connective tissue. Silver skin is the common name for elastin, a stringy gristle that does not get tender in cooking. It is easy to recognize, as it has a shiny, silvery appearance. To remove it, slide a sharp, thin blade under part of it, being careful not to remove the good meat, and cut it off in strips until it's gone.

Portioning

Cutting a large piece of meat into individual portions allows for a faster cook time and easier plating. For example, a loin roast can be cut into chops, a tenderloin made into medallions (small filets) or a leg roast sliced into cutlets. Of course, most of these can be done by the butcher, but being able to do so confidently gives you more latitude as a cook. Use a scale to accurately weigh the portions for even cooking and distribution.

Stuffing: The Great Farce

Chops, tenderloin and roasts can be filled with a stuffing to give a dish extra moisture, flavor (hello, bacon) and color (like nuts or dried fruits).

1.

POCKET: Use a thin blade to create a pocket in the chop.

2.

STUFFING: Disposable piping bags help get the stuffing into the pocket.

Unlike chicken and turkey, which have a natural cavity you can fill, for pork, you will have to create a place to put the stuffing. In the classical kitchen, a meat-based stuffing is called a "farce" or "forcemeat" and can be bound with eggs, cream or cheese. We can also make a stuffing with starchy foods like bread. Color and texture that comes by way of roasted peppers, olives, cranberries, etc., is revealed when you slice the meat open, making for a beautiful presentation. I like to put the sauce underneath a slice of roast or chop that has been stuffed so I don't hide the work that went into the filling. In addition to the variety of stuffing types, there are a number of ways to cut the meat to form the cavity.

Butterfly

Taking a piece of meat and making a series of cuts into it to open it up, called butterflying, gives you a large surface area to place the stuffing on. You can then roll it up and tie or wrap it before cooking. A trimmed whole tenderloin can be sliced lengthwise, nearly but not all the way through, so it opens up like a book. It's then placed between a cut-open resealable plastic bag, and pounded with a meat hammer to an even layer before the stuffing is added.

Pocket

Chops or boneless loin portions can be individually stuffed and then pan-roasted, sliced and sauced. One way to fill a single chop is to make a small "keyhole" incision into the loin muscle, just at the base of the rib bone, and then curve the knife in an arc to make a pocket (1). The keyhole only needs to be large enough to fit a piping bag tip, which you use to pipe in the stuffing. For this style, though, the stuffing has to be able to go through the piping tip (2). The easier, less elegant method is to simply cut through the loin to the bone or nearly through (for a boneless one) and then place the stuffing inside this pocket and fold the meat back over to cover it. These can be left as-is for roasting, secured with a toothpick or even wrapped with a strip of bacon to hold the stuffing inside.

3.

4.

PINWHEEL: A loin roast can be opened for stuffing the way you'd unroll a carpet.

Cut with one hand and unroll with the other. Take your time and don't cut through the meat.

Pinwheel

Roasts from the loin, either boneless or rack, can be opened up and stuffed to present a spiral of stuffing. The loin is butterflied, but instead of splitting it down the middle it is cut lengthwise to open up like a rolled carpet (3). The meat ends up being about ½ inch (12 mm) thick. To do this, use a sharp knife to make a cut along the length, just under the fat portion, then continue at the same angle until the whole cylinder unrolls (4). Once the meat is in a flat rectangle, place it between a cut-open resealable plastic bag, and use a meat hammer to pound and make it even and as thin as you like. Spread the stuffing across the meat, roll the meat up and hold it with string or wrap it in bacon (see Pork Loin Pinwheel Roast, page 219).

Panada

Often, I will make ground meats hold together with a mixture of bread crumbs and liquid, and sometimes egg. In classical cooking, this is called a "panada," and its function is to bind the meat together and soak up juices that would otherwise be lost in the cooking process. If you've ever made a meatloaf that shrank and ended up sitting in a loaf tin of juice, you could have used a panada. It keeps meatballs, meatloaf, terrine and the wonderful Pork-a-Leekie Pie (page 84) moist yet firm enough to slice easily.

Shaping Meats

Evenly sized portions cook at the same time so the doneness is consistent across the whole recipe. In addition to portion size, the shape of the meat can have an effect on the result. Ground meats are easily shaped and sized using a portion scoop. This is often called an ice-cream scoop and comes in different sizes, but you can quickly use it for meatballs and then reward yourself by making a batch of chocolate chip cookies (from one of Anna's books, of course!). For meatloaf, you can use a tin to shape the mixture into a form or a log that can be roasted alone or wrapped in bacon.

5.

CUTLETS: Flatten under an opened bag to contain any mess.

6.

TYING: This maintains the shape of the roast and holds the stuffing inside.

Burger patties are best weighed, rolled into a ball and pressed between a cut-open resealable plastic bag to the diameter of the bun, with an even thickness all around.

Cutlets

If I'm making cutlets, schnitzel or tonkatsu, I will cut the meat into portions and then place them between layers of plastic wrap or a cut-open resealable plastic bag and gently pound it to an even, thin sheet (5). They can then be coated in bread crumbs before frying or used to wrap around a stuffing in a ball shape like Leg Cutlet "Tartufi" (page 175).

Tying

Butcher's twine is a food-friendly cotton string used to hold meat together in the right shape or to tie around a roast to hold in the stuffing (6). Use a series of lengths wrapped around the meat and tied individually or practice a butcher's knot to make one continuous string looped across and tightened over a whole roast.

Marinating

The word "marinade" comes from the root word "marin" or seawater, suggesting a process of washing or soaking meat in saltwater prior to cooking. Originally, this likely cleaned and preserved the meat a little, but over time, the process grew to include spices, herbs, garlic, wine, vinegar and any other flavor imaginable. A marinade has two purposes: to add flavor to food and to tenderize tough cuts. Adding flavor makes sense (whether the contact is 10 minutes or overnight), and pork is a wonderful sponge, soaking up whatever ingredients it comes in contact with, wet or dry. Acidic liquids like wine and vinegar are added to penetrate the meat and start to break down connective tissues. The general rule is that the longer you use a marinade, the more it will penetrate the meat, but often, a quick turnaround time is fine. The marinades in the Pork Sirloin Vindaloo (page 158) and Braised Country Style Ribs (page 225) will highly season the meats and will be strongest if left for a full 12 hours.

SEASONING

Salt is the most basic vehicle to change ingredients into food, but it is also the most misunderstood. We know that too much salt should be avoided, but we also want our food to taste great. Most recipes say to "season to taste," which is problematic, as we don't want to oversalt. After all, you can always add more, but it is nearly impossible to remove. And consider the reason we add salt—its function is to make the food taste like itself. Properly seasoned pork should taste like pork, not salt. Seasoned cooks (ha ha) like me have an instinct for salt, so I can grab a pinch that starts off small and then correct just before serving, but that knowledge is developed only after years of practice. In many of the recipes in this book, I suggest a measured amount of salt to use, but this is always subject to your own taste. Generally, if salt is less than 1% of the weight of the food, you won't even be able to taste it, but once it goes over 2.5%, the food tastes too salty. This is when you wake up at 3 a.m. needing a glass of water. A lot of processed foods are too salty for me. I have found that most of my cooking is enjoyed best at 1.7% salt by weight. However, I recognize that using percentages is a challenge for home cooking, as the quantities are not that great, and we don't necessarily have accurate scales that measure to such fine amounts. I am not going to calculate to the milligram if I'm making a little lunch for two people, but if I was making a huge amount of meatloaf or sausage in a commercial kitchen, I would be able to figure out how much salt to start off with. For example, if I was using 220 lb (100 kg) of ground meat for meatloaf or meatballs, I could calculate that it requires around 3.7 lb (1.7 kg) of salt to get to the desired 1.7%.

At home, I find the best way to succeed is to taste the food as I am cooking. The last thing I do before serving any food is to taste for salt and add more if necessary. If you are reducing the amount of sodium in your diet, you can look to herbs, acid and chilies to pick up the slack—a squeeze of lemon or squirt of hot sauce can wake up dishes the same way salt does.

Types of Salt

Table salt is the most common. It's ground finely enough to pass through a restaurant-style salt shaker and is sprinkled onto foods or added to water to cook pasta and vegetables. Table salt traditionally has a small amount of iodine added to it (it's easy to develop a thyroid problem from a lack of iodine, so this is a preventive measure).

Table salt dissolves easily and is used in baking for this reason, but many cooks, myself included, like to use salt by pinching it with their fingers, so they prefer a coarser salt that has a distinct feel to it, making it easier to know how much you are using. I always found that table salt sticks under my fingernails and melts if my hands are at all wet. Regardless of what type of salt you use, remember that all of them have the same amount of sodium by weight, so a gram of table salt has the same amount of sodium as a gram of kosher salt, for example. But the texture makes a difference in volume, so there is more salt in 1 tablespoon (30 mL) of table salt than there is in 1 tablespoon (30 mL) of kosher salt, because of the shape of the crystals.

In the recipes found in this book, you'll see I approach salt in two ways. When I'm calling for a specific measurement, I'll tell you the type of salt to use. In other instances, you'll just see "salt" mentioned in the ingredients list. Here, I encourage you to use your own judgment and choose whichever salt you prefer. Below is a list of the types of salt I use most often.

- **Kosher salt** is a flaked variety used in "koshering" meats to remove blood but is popular with many chefs as it does not melt or stick to the fingers. It doesn't dissolve into food right away, so you can see it on meats and vegetables.

- **Coarse pickling salt** is a form of salt with no iodine added to it, as many pickle recipes containing garlic will turn a pale blue in the presence of iodine. I like this salt for seasoning meat because of the feel on my fingers—I know exactly how much I'm adding. I don't use it for the baking powder–salt mix mentioned on page 251 because the granule size is so much bigger than the baking powder.

- **Finishing salts** have either a particular point of origin (Himalayan Pink, Hawaiian Red) or a specific process (Maldon, or Fleur de Sel from Camargue, France) that is used for color or texture. They are very expensive compared to other salts and are used only as a finishing touch on dishes. You wouldn't use them for salted pasta water but you could sprinkle them over ripe garden tomatoes. These salts do not dissolve right away, so they have a distinctive crunch when you bite the food.

- **Curing salt** is used by professional butchers, meat processors and basement salami enthusiasts. It's also called pink salt or Prague powder. It has a small percentage of sodium nitrite added to it to act as a preservative and keep the meat pink as it cures, instead of turning a gray color. This salt also has a red dye added (unlike Himalayan Pink salt) to give it a distinct color so it does not get mixed up with regular salt.

NOTE: Salt is present in countless food products, one of which is butter. For the purposes of this book, unless specified otherwise, all recipes should be made with unsalted butter. This will allow you to control the seasoning as you see fit.

LET'S GO TO THE STOVE

When I plan a meal for company or any large gathering, I write down the menu and then come up with a to-do list organized chronologically. This is my prep list, and it ensures I will get everything done in time for dinner. Here's a basic example: you would start your roast well ahead of setting the table or making the tossed salad. It may sound like an overly simplistic idea, but it makes sense to lay out the day (or days, depending on what you're making and whether it can be done ahead of time) in terms of how long things will take to prepare.

Meat has to be stored in the fridge, for obvious reasons, but I will take it out before cooking to take the chill off it. For small cuts like chops or steaks, this might be 15 minutes, but for a roast, it could be 30 to 45 minutes. The other thing I do is to pat the meat dry with paper towel if it is really moist from the packaging. You'll find this in the case of vacuum-packed meats. The pressure inside the packaging draws water out of the meat and it just has to be wiped clean. Browning the meat is much easier if it starts off dry.

Searing

Browning meat in hot fat sets the color to a deep golden brown and helps develop rich flavors in the meat and sauce. This is called the Maillard reaction. For most pan-fried or stewed items, you'll want to achieve this color before you proceed with the cooking. Put a small amount of fat into the skillet and heat over high until the oil sputters if you touch any meat to it. Ensuring that the meat is dry, season it with salt and add to the pan. Place the meat down away from you so the oil won't splash back toward you. Leave it alone for 1 to 2 minutes and then turn it over to color the other side. Be patient and give the meat enough time to brown, and it will not stick to the pan when you try to turn it. Once it's browned, you can turn the heat down to medium to cook through or finish cooking the meat in the oven. You may have to do this in a few batches if you are cooking several portions—you want to keep the pan as hot as possible, so don't do too much at once.

Sweating

When starting off a soup or stew, you sometimes want to cook the aromatic vegetables together to release their flavors without developing color, especially in the case of a light-colored finished dish. Cook the onions or other vegetables over medium heat in a little fat with the lid on until the onions turn translucent and the aroma develops.

Sautéing

Picture someone cooking a dish in a hot pan, constantly flipping sizzling pieces of food in the

air. This "jump frying" is what I mean by the term "sauté." You can cook a complete dish in minutes using this method. To do this, you'll want a high heat source and a good pan for browning bite-sized pieces of food. Try this on Caramelized Chili Pork with Peanuts & Lime (page 141). You can also sauté to start cooking the aromatic flavor builders for a stew or chili before the liquid is added.

Pan-Frying

Pan-frying is great for cooking portions (like chops) on the stovetop in oil or butter, usually only flipping once (compared to sautéing, in which you are always moving the food). To pan-fry, make sure the meat is patted dry and seasoned with salt and pepper, and then heat the pan with the oil or butter over high heat to get the initial sear (as described in *Searing* above). The heat can be reduced to cook the item through, depending on the thickness. I don't cover the pan (it will steam the food) or add liquid, as the development of a golden brown crust is ideal. To make several items, like schnitzels, I will cook them in batches, say, two at a time, and then set them on a baking sheet and keep them warm in the oven. For thick items, you can start the browning on the stovetop and then finish cooking in the oven—this is called pan-roasting. The oven provides a surrounding

heat rather than heating just from the bottom of the pan. Once the meat is cooked by either of these two methods, you can deglaze the pan.

Deglazing

After browning meat or aromatics or after pan-roasting meats, there will be a bit of caramelization or "fond" on the pan, and it has a lot of flavor. To release the fond, you remove excess fat from the pan and then add a small amount of cool liquid, often wine, to turn the brown bits into a liquid state. Scrape the bottom of the pan with a wooden spoon as you add the liquid, and you will have an intensely flavorful "pan jus." You can add this to an existing sauce or use it as a starting point for a new one. Effective cooking is all about getting the most potential out of each ingredient and not wasting anything. Although this little technique may seem inconsequential, it is absolutely worth the effort.

Braising

Less tender cuts of meat (usually those cuts that are from the lower part of the animal) need low, moist heat to break down the connective tissues in the muscle. Use a combination of searing and adding liquid to bring these cuts to a fully cooked but moist and tender texture. While quick-cooked chops and steaks are often fairly straightforward in terms of ingredients, braising can layer in levels of complex flavor by adding aromatics and seasonings to the braising liquid (see Braised Sirloin with Peppers, Chili & Chocolate, page 222).

Deep-Frying

Deep-frying is when the item is submerged entirely in hot oil (around 350°F/180°C) so that there is no contact with the pot or pan. Oil gets nearly twice as hot as boiling water, so I always encourage caution. I rarely deep-fry at home because it can be messy, it may leave a lingering aroma and it can be dangerous. However, it can produce some really tasty dishes, so when I want to deep-fry something, I compromise and use a tabletop deep fryer outside in warm weather. There is also a technique called shallow frying, in which food is immersed in about 2 inches (5 cm) of oil. I use a Dutch oven with a thermometer to ensure proper temperature and safety. Do not leave hot oil unattended.

Roasting

The oven is a wonderful tool for roasting meats, especially when you are cooking for a crowd, because it is hands-off. Cooking and carving one large piece of meat is less stressful than making individual portions for everyone. For roasting smaller amounts, I like to use a baking sheet lined with parchment paper or foil (for easy cleanup) and a rack set overtop (for airflow around the whole piece). A large roast can go directly into a roasting pan, and the sauce can be made right in the pan after the meat is cooked. In some cases, you will brown the meat first, but for larger roasts, I simply season and put it straight into the oven. Use either an instant-read or digital thermometer to keep an eye on the temperature.

BASTING: As juices come out of the meat during cooking, spoon them over the surface of the roast to encourage a golden brown exterior and a moist interior.

GLAZING: If you want to add a sweet, sticky finishing glaze to meat, add it toward the end of cooking. If you put a sugary sauce on too early, it will scorch and might taste bitter. This is a nice way to finish off a ham or meatloaf (see Bacon Wrapped Meatloaf with Orange Marmalade & Beer Glaze, page 145), as it adds incredible flavor and produces a shiny, juicy-looking outside.

RESTING: I allow for a rest period after a roast comes out of the oven. When the meat is hot, the liquid in its cells is likely to leak out if the meat is sliced immediately. A 5-minute rest on the cutting board will let the meat juices settle and stay in the meat rather than end up on your board. Remember that a roast will continue to cook by several degrees after it comes out of the oven, so you can remove, rest and even put it back into the oven to gently reheat. When I cook for a gang, I'll do something like the Boneless Loin in Black Pepper Mustard with Welland Market Relish (page 240)—while the meat is roasting, I prepare the sauce and remove the roast before I need to carve and serve. I just need a 5-minute window to heat the roast and sauce, and I can tell stories in the meantime.

Carving

The glory of a roast is being able to carve it in front of your guests like the proud parent in a Norman Rockwell painting—it's a beautiful representation of sharing and expressing care through food. Set up your station with a large cutting board, a platter and a sauceboat, a bowl for trim or bones, and a carving fork and long knife. Keep a kitchen towel nearby for your hands, and remove any clutter in the immediate area. Carve in broad strokes across the grain of the meat, and use your fork and knife or a set of tongs to serve the slices or lay them across a platter. I like to put a little bit of sauce with the meat but also serve sauce on the side for those who want more. Start with just a small portion if you are serving on individual plates, as it's easy enough to carve seconds and the meat will stay juicier if it's left whole. And, of course, as the chef, you have every right to sneak little bits of brown edges when no one is looking—for quality-control purposes, of course.

Cooking Bacon

Although bacon can be a stand-alone food item for breakfast or in sandwiches, it is used as an ingredient or flavor builder throughout this book. It brings salty, meaty and smoky tastes to just about anything and can provide a wonderful crunch for texture. It can be purchased sliced, in a slab, flavored, double-smoked or as pancetta (Italian-style rolled, not smoked). If I need to thinly slice or dice it, I do so while the bacon is cold, straight from the refrigerator.

PAN-FRYING: Lay strips of bacon in a skillet and pan-fry over medium heat to crisp up on both sides. Remove the bacon to a plate lined with paper towel to drain excess fat. To make bacon bits, you can either dice cooked, drained bacon or dice the uncooked bacon first and cook over medium heat until crisp and then drain. Avoid cooking over high heat, as it will scorch the bacon.

OVEN BAKING: If you need a lot of bacon, lay out the strips on a parchment paper–lined baking sheet and cook in a 350°F (180°C) oven for 30 minutes or until golden, flipping the bacon over halfway through cooking. You can also use a bacon rack, which suspends the bacon to allow fat to melt away and keep the bacon from curling while cooking.

GRILLING: For an outdoor breakfast, you can put a baking sheet (use an old one, trust me) right on the grill or you can use thick-cut bacon seasoned with BBQ rub and directly grill it over medium heat.

LARDONS: Slab bacon (with the skin removed) can be cut into ¼-inch (6 mm) batons, blanched for 1 minute in boiling water and then pan fried crisp to add to a salad. This removes a bit of salt and fat but makes the bacon really firm to the bite (see Bacon & Egg Salad on Bitter Greens with Red Wine Vinaigrette & Croutons, page 39).

THE DELI COUNTER

OLSON HARDWARE

MODEL: 100 U.S. Slicing Machine   **MANUFACTURER**: Berkel   **YEAR**: 1918

NOTES: Van Berkel invented the meat slicer in Holland back in 1898 to make bacon slicing more efficient. He later opened plants in the United States, Canada and Argentina.

Naples Breakfast

Prosciutto with Peaches & Ricotta Cheese

On our first trip to Italy, Anna and I would eat in our little hotel dining room each morning, grinning ear to ear just at the prospect of being in Naples. To our delight, the kitchen set out a very simple make-your-own buffet, and there were single-portion crocks of freshly made ricotta cheese alongside the prosciutto and summer peaches. We recreate this dish often during our local peach season in Niagara, Ontario, with locally made ham and cheese. *Buon giorno!*

12 thin slices best-quality prosciutto

3 ripe peaches, peeled and sliced

1 cup (250 mL) creamy ricotta cheese (any fat percentage)

8 fresh basil leaves

4-8 slices thick country bread, toasted

1 Arrange the prosciutto and peach slices on a serving plate and spoon the ricotta into a bowl. Sprinkle the plate with the basil leaves and serve with the bread.

2 To eat, spread a generous amount of ricotta on the bread and top with prosciutto, peach slices and basil leaves.

Notes:

+ Peel the peaches just before slicing to keep them juicy and from turning brown, or toss the peaches in a little lemon juice if preparing ahead.

Warm Prosciutto & Brie Wrapped Asparagus

with Red Pepper Sauce

34

RED PEPPER SAUCE

2 tsp (10 mL) olive oil

1 red bell pepper, seeded and roughly chopped

1 shallot, minced

½ cup (125 mL) chicken stock

Salt

ASPARAGUS

24 slender asparagus spears

4 oz (120 g) Brie cheese

12 thin slices prosciutto

¼ cup (60 mL) finely grated Parmigiano-Reggiano

¼ cup (60 mL) plain dry bread crumbs

2 Tbsp (30 mL) olive oil

Chopped fresh Italian parsley, for garnish

We like to go hog wild over seasonal ingredients in Niagara, and asparagus is the real harbinger of the local growing season. In our cooking, asparagus will appear three times a day for 1 month, and then we basically say goodbye for the rest of the year (OK, we cheat and buy imported in February). This is a great pass-around appetizer for when dinner guests arrive.

1 For the sauce, heat the oil in a small saucepot over medium heat. Add the bell pepper and shallot, and sauté until the bell pepper is softened, about 3 minutes. Add the chicken stock and simmer until the bell pepper is tender, about 10 minutes. Puree the mixture using an immersion blender or food processor, and season to taste. Keep warm over low heat until ready to serve, or prepare ahead, chill and reheat over low heat before serving.

2 Preheat the oven to 325°F (160°C) and line a baking sheet with parchment paper.

3 Trim the bottoms of the asparagus about 1 inch (2.5 cm) to remove the tough part. Portion the Brie into 12 thin slices.

4 Lay a slice of prosciutto on a cutting board and top with 2 asparagus spears on a diagonal, then top with a slice of Brie (1). Roll the prosciutto up and around the asparagus and Brie, making a bundle (2). Place the bundles on the prepared baking sheet, 1 inch (2.5 cm) apart, and repeat with the remaining prosciutto, Brie and asparagus.

5 Stir together the Parmigiano-Reggiano, bread crumbs and olive oil, then sprinkle the mixture over the prosciutto bundles (3). Bake until the bread crumbs are golden brown and crisp, about 20 minutes.

6 To serve, spoon about ¼ cup (60 mL) of the red pepper sauce on each plate, top with 3 prosciutto bundles and sprinkle with parsley. Serve immediately.

Notes:

+ The red pepper sauce also makes a delicious, full-flavored but low-fat dressing for salads or vegetables. You can also try this recipe with a different cheese, like Oka, chèvre or blue.

1.

2.

3.

Prosciutto & Melon

with Basil & Grissini

This classic from the Italian kitchen is such a great way to show off quality ham, as the salty character of the meat is balanced by the sweetness of the melon. Serve it as a shared appetizer or part of an antipasto buffet.

16 thin slices prosciutto
1 ripe cantaloupe
16 fresh basil leaves
16 Italian breadsticks

37

1   Loosely arrange the prosciutto on one half of a large platter or cutting board. Avoid rolling the prosciutto up into parcels. Instead, lay it out in ruffles so it takes up a lot of space—it is much tastier when it melts over your tongue instead of being chewed.

2   Wash and peel the whole melon using a chef's knife, and then cut it in half lengthwise and scoop out the seeds. Cut each half into 8 half-moon pieces and arrange them next to the prosciutto. Tear the basil leaves with your fingers and sprinkle over the cantaloupe slices. Chill until ready to serve.

3   To serve, place the breadsticks beside the prosciutto and melon platter, and let guests either wrap the prosciutto around the breadsticks or over the melon to enjoy the sweet and salty balance.

Notes:

+ Add a little fresh lime juice to the melon if it is out of season and not as ripe as you hoped. The contrast of the lime heightens the sweetness of the melon.

+ If you want to make your own breadsticks, buy pizza dough, cut into 1½-inch (4 cm) rounds, roll into pencil shapes and bake at 400°F (200°C) until crisp, about 15 minutes.

Bacon & Egg Salad on Bitter Greens

with Red Wine Vinaigrette & Croutons

A classic French bistro standard, the poached egg and frisée make a wonderful frame for the chewy nuggets of smoked slab bacon, which is cut into little sticks and blanched before frying. These are not bacon bits—these are lardons. The first time you try this recipe, the timing will be a challenge, but it gets easier.

1   Cut the bacon into "batons"—2 x ¼ inch (5 cm x 6 mm) sticks. Bring a small saucepot of water to a rolling boil over high heat and drop in the bacon to blanch for 1 minute and then drain. Heat a sauté pan over medium heat, add the blanched bacon and sauté until crisp, about 5 minutes. Remove the bacon to a plate lined with paper towel.

2   For the croutons, preheat the oven to 350°F (180°C) and line a baking sheet with parchment paper. Toss the diced baguette in a large bowl with the olive oil, garlic, salt and pepper, arrange on the prepared baking sheet and toast until golden brown, about 10 minutes.

3   For the poached eggs, bring 4 cups (1 L) water to a gentle boil over medium-high heat in a medium saucepot. Add the vinegar and reduce to a bare simmer. Stir with a spoon to create a cyclone effect in the water. Crack an egg into a small dish, and gently tip into the water. Repeat with the remaining eggs, dropping them in one at a time, and cooking until the white is firm but the yolk is still runny, about 3 minutes. Gently lift each egg from the water using a slotted spoon and place on a paper towel to drain.

4   For the dressing, whisk the vinegar, shallot, parsley and mustard with 1 Tbsp (15 mL) water in a bowl. Pour in the oil in a steady stream while whisking until incorporated. Season with salt and pepper, and keep covered in the fridge until ready to use, up to 5 days.

5   To serve, dress the frisée lettuce with the red wine vinaigrette, season with salt and pepper, and arrange on individual plates. Top with bacon, croutons and poached eggs.

½ lb (225 g) double-smoked bacon

½ baguette, cut in 1-inch (2.5 cm) dice

1 Tbsp (15 mL) olive oil

1 clove garlic, minced

Salt and pepper

4 large eggs

1 Tbsp (15 mL) white wine vinegar

4 cups (1 L) frisée lettuce, trimmed, washed and cut in bite-sized pieces

¼ cup (60 mL) Red Wine Vinaigrette

RED WINE VINAIGRETTE

¼ cup (60 mL) red wine vinegar

½ shallot, minced

2 Tbsp (30 mL) finely chopped fresh Italian parsley

1 tsp (5 mL) Dijon mustard

⅔ cup (160 mL) extra virgin olive oil

Salt and pepper

Notes:

+ Frisée has a frilly leaf that catches the dressing, and its slightly bitter character stands up to the bacon. If you can't find frisée, use Belgian endive, arugula or escarole.

YIELD: 4 SERVINGS
MAKES ONE 12-INCH
(2.5 L) CASSEROLE

PREP TIME:
10 MINUTES

COOK TIME:
2 HOURS, 15 MINUTES

Sausage Cassoulet

Our visit to the French town of Carcassonne, the home of cassoulet, was all about eating this dish near the medieval fortress. It was a blazing hot summer day, and after finishing a big portion, I was ready to storm the castle. Local legend tells of a princess who, under siege, made a move that was a gamble. The attackers planned to starve the occupants out, but she used a catapult to launch the last pig they had, as a sign of defiance. The invaders, seeing what she had done, assumed there were enough stores to last, so they gave up and left. The original recipe for cassoulet calls for duck confit, a delicious but uncommon ingredient, so I go the all-sausage route—hey, I'm busy storming castles, after all.

---

1   Preheat the oven to 350°F (180°C).

2   Cut each of the fresh sausages into 4 pieces and dice the bacon into bite-sized pieces. Heat a large skillet over medium-high heat and cook the sausages and bacon until golden brown, about 5 minutes. Add the onion, carrots, celery, thyme and garlic, and sauté, reducing the heat to medium if the onion starts to brown, until the onion starts to soften, 3 to 5 minutes. Spoon the meat mixture into a 12-inch (2.5 L) casserole dish.

3   Stir the diced tomatoes and beans together and pour over the meat mixture. Add enough stock to reach the top of the beans, then sprinkle an even layer of the bread crumbs overtop. Bake, uncovered, until the top has a golden brown crust and the juices are bubbling, about 2 hours.

4   To serve, ladle the cassoulet into bowls along with a side salad and a crispy baguette, and maybe serve it with a bottle of light red or rosé wine.

1 lb (450 g) fresh honey garlic or mild Italian sausages

4 oz (120 g) slab smoked bacon

1 medium onion, diced

2 carrots, peeled and diced

2 stalks celery, diced

2 tsp (10 mL) chopped fresh thyme

2 cloves garlic, minced

1 can (19 oz/ 540 mL) diced tomatoes

2 cans (each 19 oz/ 540 mL) white kidney beans, drained and rinsed

2 cups (500 mL) chicken stock

1/3 cup (160 mL) dry bread crumbs (not panko)

Notes:

+   I like to use a broad, open casserole dish to get the most out of the crust that develops on top. Once it comes out of the oven, it will stay hot for 20 minutes.

Lynn Lake Breakfast

with Bacon, Cheddar & Stewed Tomatoes

4 large thick slices
   rustic bread

1 cup (250 mL) coarsely
   grated cheddar cheese

1 can (28 oz/796 mL) diced
   stewed tomatoes

8 slices thick-cut bacon,
   cooked and drained

Salt and pepper

2 Tbsp (30 mL) chopped
   fresh Italian parsley

My Aunt Hazel ruled the roost in a small northern Manitoba mining town called Lynn Lake. She was known for this breakfast dish of bacon-topped cheese toast with stewed tomatoes—if you simply say "Lynn Lake" to any of my six siblings, this rare treat is what they picture.

———————

1   Preheat the oven to 350°F (180°C) and line a baking sheet with parchment paper. Arrange the bread slices on the tray and toast until lightly browned, 10 to 15 minutes. Top the toasted bread with the cheese and return to the oven until the cheese has melted, 5 to 8 minutes. While the toasts are in the oven, bring the stewed tomatoes up to a full simmer in a saucepot over medium heat, stirring occasionally.

2   To serve, ladle a generous amount of stewed tomatoes on a plate, add a cheese toast, top with 2 slices of the cooked bacon, then a little more of the stewed tomatoes. To finish, sprinkle with chopped parsley.

Notes:

+ If you're feeding a crowd, make and bake the cheese toasts just before guests arrive and then reheat on a tray. For a slightly different take, try this recipe with sliced double-smoked or cooked peameal bacon.

Ham Waldorf Salad

Waldorf is so old, it's new again. This classic is a wonderful addition to a holiday brunch or family gathering (and I like to use those delicious bits of leftover ham). The richness of the dressing against the tart apples and grapes is a perfect backdrop for the smoky ham.

1   In a large mixing bowl, whisk the mayonnaise, yogurt and lemon juice until smooth. Stir in the ham, apple, celery, grapes, walnuts, chives, salt and pepper. Cover and refrigerate until ready to serve.

2   To assemble, use the larger lettuce leaves to line the platter and tear the remaining inner leaves into the salad. Toss to coat, then spoon onto the platter and serve.

¼ cup (60 mL) mayonnaise

¼ cup (60 mL) plain yogurt

1 Tbsp (15 mL) fresh lemon juice

1 cup (250 mL) diced cooked ham

1 unpeeled apple (I like Honey Crisp), cored and diced

2 stalks celery, diced

1 cup (250 mL) halved seedless green grapes

½ cup (125 mL) lightly toasted walnut pieces

2 Tbsp (30 mL) chopped fresh chives

Salt and pepper

1 head Boston lettuce, washed and trimmed

45

THE DELI COUNTER

Notes:

+   To toast the walnuts, cook in a single layer over medium heat in a dry skillet, stirring often, to wake up the aromas, just over 5 minutes. Keep your eye on the pan so they don't scorch.

Chorizo Manchego Stuffed Dates

12 Medjool dates

12 bite-sized pieces Spanish chorizo salami

2 piquillo peppers or roasted red peppers, cut in 12 bite-sized pieces

2 oz (60 g) Manchego cheese, cut in 12 bite-sized pieces

We love the tapas culture when visiting Barcelona, and there are now so many more quality Spanish ingredients available in supermarkets and specialty shops in North America. The real key to making this tasty morsel is using the Medjool dates—soft, sweet and savory, they're the perfect container for the cheese, peppers and chorizo!

1 Preheat the oven to 375°F (190°C).

2 Make a lengthwise slice in each date, remove the pit and stuff with a piece each of the chorizo, pepper and cheese. Lay the dates, stuffed side up, on an ungreased pie plate and warm in the oven, until the cheese melts but does not leak out, 8 to 10 minutes. They can be served warm from the oven on a platter.

Notes:

+ A good rule for figuring out how many tapas to make for a gathering is to plan on 2 or 3 of these per person with 2 drinks.

YIELD: MAKES
ABOUT 3 DOZEN
SHORTBREAD

PREP TIME:
10 MINUTES,
PLUS CHILLING

COOK TIME:
18 MINUTES

Bacon Cheddar Shortbread

One of the many things I respect about Anna's cooking is her ability to seamlessly move back and forth from the pastry kitchen to the savory line. It's not easy, but her classical training and experience in the hot kitchen makes it look effortless. If you thought shortbread was only for the sweet table, take a look at these.

1   Preheat the oven to 300°F (150°C). Lightly grease and line an 8-inch (20 cm) square pan with parchment paper so the paper comes up and hangs over the sides.

2   Using a food processor, pulse the bacon with the flour, sugar and pepper until the bacon is finely chopped. Add the butter and pulse until blended, then add the cheese and pulse until the dough comes together. Press the dough into the prepared pan and dock it with a fork (this promotes even baking).

3   Bake the shortbread for about 30 minutes, until the edges begin to brown slightly. Set the pan onto a cooling rack and cut the shortbread into squares while it is still hot, then let it cool completely in the pan before removing. The shortbread will keep for up to 1 week in an air-tight container.

3 strips smoked bacon, cooked and drained

1 cup + 6 Tbsp (340 mL) all-purpose flour

2 tsp (10 mL) granulated sugar

¼ tsp (1 mL) ground black pepper

6 Tbsp (90 g) cold butter, cut in pieces

4 oz (120 g) coarsely grated old cheddar cheese (about 1⅓ cups)

Notes:

+ This pastry is wonderful for lining savory tart shells, such as the Butternut Squash, Bacon & Cheddar Tart (page 50). You can also switch out the cheddar in this recipe with a cheese of similar texture, such as Asiago or a young Gouda.

YIELD: 10 SERVINGS
MAKES ONE 9-INCH
(23 CM) TART

PREP TIME:
15 MINUTES,
PLUS CHILLING

COOK TIME: 1 HOUR,
PLUS RESTING

Butternut Squash, Bacon & Cheddar Tart

1 recipe Bacon Cheddar Shortbread dough (page 49), shaped into a disc and chilled

1½ cups (375 mL) thawed frozen butternut squash puree

4 large eggs

½ tsp (2 mL) fine salt

¼ tsp (1 mL) ground black pepper

1½ cups (375 mL) coarsely grated old cheddar cheese

8 slices bacon, cooked, drained and crumbled

3 green onions, thinly sliced

I don't bake often, but I love to make treats for Anna (and get her help), so I found a use for one of her delicious doughs: as a base for this tart. It's completely open to variations, so you can use up bacon, ham or even leftover BBQ pork. You can make the filling with fresh or frozen squash, and the tart looks so good coming out of the oven, you won't be able to let it cool down before trying a slice.

---

1 Preheat the oven to 350°F (180°C).

2 On a lightly floured surface, roll out the dough into a circle just under ¼ inch (6 mm) thick. Line a 9-inch (23 cm) fluted tart pan with a removable bottom with the pastry. Press the pastry into the edges of the pan and trim away the excess. Dock the bottom of the pastry (by pricking it with a fork) and chill for 30 minutes.

3 Place the tart pan on a baking sheet and bake until the pastry loses its shine and browns just a little at the edges, about 15 minutes. Let the tray cool on a rack while preparing the filling.

4 Whisk the butternut squash puree with the eggs, salt and pepper until evenly combined and then stir in the cheese, bacon and green onions. Pour the mixture into the cooled tart shell and bake, still at 350°F (180°C), until the filling no longer jiggles in the center, about 45 minutes. Let the tart cool for at least 15 minutes before slicing to serve.

Notes:

+ If you're making your own butternut squash puree, you can use either fresh or frozen squash. Simply boil it until tender, drain well and puree until smooth. Serve this dish with salad as a light lunch or as a starter for a fancy dinner (don't worry, no one will notice when you sneak a slice right out of the fridge).

Braised Endives

with Gruyère & Black Forest Ham

Endives often appear on salads, but they are a really great cooked side dish, especially when married with ham and cheese in a creamy wine sauce—you'll think you're dining in the Swiss Alps when you try these. I love serving this dish either as an appetizer course or as a side for family-style dinners where the table looks like a buffet, with all the different platters and casseroles served at once.

1   For the béchamel, melt the butter in a medium saucepot over medium heat. Stir in the shallots and cook for about 5 minutes to soften the shallots but not brown them. Stir in the flour and cook, stirring constantly with a wooden spoon (still over medium heat), until the flour starts to take on the aroma of almonds but does not turn brown, 3 to 5 minutes. Slowly pour in the milk while whisking, then add the nutmeg. Bring the sauce up to a full simmer while whisking before adding the wine. Season to taste and set aside. The sauce can be prepped ahead of time, chilled and then reheated to a simmer over medium-low heat before assembling the dish

2   Preheat the oven to 400°F (200°C) and lightly grease a casserole dish.

3   Cut the Belgian endives lengthwise into quarters (or halves if small) and wrap each quarter with a slice of the Black Forest ham. Lay them closely together in the casserole dish. Spoon the béchamel sauce over the endives and sprinkle the cheese in an even layer overtop. Bake until the top of the dish is golden brown, the sauce is bubbling and the endives are fork-tender, 20 to 25 minutes.

4   Serve immediately, topped with the parsley.

BÉCHAMEL SAUCE

¼ cup (60 mL) butter

2 Tbsp (30 mL) minced shallots (about 1 shallot)

¼ cup (60 mL) all-purpose flour

2 cups (500 mL) 2% milk

Pinch ground nutmeg

½ cup (125 mL) dry white wine

Salt

ENDIVE

2 large or 4 small heads Belgian endive

8 slices deli-style Black Forest ham

1 cup (250 mL) coarsely grated Gruyère cheese

2 Tbsp (30 mL) chopped fresh Italian parsley

Notes:

+   Choose endives that are tightly closed and bright white with yellow (not green) tips. The green tips mean they've been exposed to sunlight and might taste too bitter.

YIELD: 6 SERVINGS
MAKES ONE 10-INCH
(25 CM) TART

PREP TIME:
10 MINUTES

COOK TIME:
65 MINUTES,
PLUS RESTING

Bacon Onion Tart

with Balsamic & Tomatoes

1 Tbsp (15 mL) butter or reserved drippings from the cooked bacon

2 yellow onions, sliced

Splash balsamic vinegar

1 tsp (5 mL) chopped fresh thyme leaves

Salt and pepper

1 sheet (8 oz/225 g) frozen butter puff pastry, thawed in the fridge

6 slices bacon, cooked, drained and crumbled

12 cherry tomatoes, halved

Cut into bites for a perfect appetizer or served as a slice for a starter course, this tart pleases everyone and might become a family favorite. Just a few ingredients baked on crisp pastry will have your guests wondering if there aren't a bunch of secret ingredients at work here. The balsamic glazed onions have a rich, meaty aroma and the bacon, well, I mean, it's bacon!

1   Melt the butter in a large sauté pan over medium heat, then stir in the onions. Sauté the onions until they turn a golden brown and their volume reduces by half, about 35 minutes. Add the balsamic vinegar and stir the onions with a wooden spoon to pull up the caramelized bits from the pan. Stir in the thyme, season to taste and then remove the pan from the heat and let cool at room temperature. This can be made up to a day ahead and chilled until ready to assemble.

2   Preheat the oven to 400°F (200°C) and line a baking sheet with parchment paper.

3   Lay the sheet of puff pastry on the baking sheet and dock it with a fork across the surface (this prevents it from rising too much). Spread the cooled onions in an even layer over the pastry, right to the edges, and sprinkle the crumbled bacon overtop. Arrange the cherry tomato halves overtop in 4 rows of 6. Bake the tart until it is puffed and golden brown at the edges, about 30 minutes.

4   To serve, transfer the baking sheet to a cooling rack for 5 minutes, then cut the pastry into 24 pieces so that a cherry tomato half is on each piece. Pick up with your fingers to eat warm or at room temperature.

Notes:

+   Puff pastry needs a hot oven to make it crisp, light and airy, so be sure to fully heat it to temperature before baking.

Potato Soup

with Pancetta, Peas & Ricotta Cheese

This warming soup can be served chilled in warm weather but really hits home on a cold autumn day. It's only made more complete with a grilled cheese sandwich and an afternoon nap!

1   Heat a large saucepot over medium heat and fry the pancetta for about 5 minutes to crisp up. Remove the pancetta with a slotted spoon to a plate lined with paper towel to drain, but keep any drippings in the pot.

2   Add the onion to the pot and sauté until translucent, about 5 minutes. Add the stock, potatoes and thyme to the pot, and bring to a boil over medium heat. Reduce the heat to medium-low, cover the pot and gently simmer until the potatoes crush easily when pressed with a spoon, about 20 minutes.

3   Remove the pot from the heat and use an immersion blender to puree the mixture until smooth. Return the pot to medium heat, stir in the reserved pancetta, peas and cream. Bring the soup back to a simmer and season to taste.

4   To serve, ladle the soup into bowls and top each with a dollop of ricotta and a sprinkling of chives.

⅓ cup (80 mL) diced pancetta

½ medium yellow onion, sliced

4 cups (1 L) chicken stock

2 cups (500 mL) peeled and diced Yukon Gold or russet potatoes

2 tsp (10 mL) fresh thyme leaves

½ cup (125 mL) frozen peas

½ cup (125 mL) 35% whipping cream

Salt and pepper

⅓ cup (80 mL) creamy ricotta cheese

2 Tbsp (30 mL) chopped fresh chives

Notes:

+   Be sure to use large potatoes for a creamy consistency, not the "new" little ones, as they will have a sticky texture when pureed.

White Bean Soup with Bacon & Lemon

4 slices bacon, diced

1 medium yellow onion, diced

1 clove garlic, minced

2 cans (each 19 oz/540 mL) white kidney beans

1 lemon

3½ cups (875 mL) water or chicken stock

Salt and pepper

1 Tbsp (15 mL) chopped fresh Italian parsley or chives

This soup will taste like it took hours of simmering, but it comes together in a snap, and you can have it on the table in less time than it takes to watch the news on TV. Some of the beans and bacon are held back from the puree to add a nice texture in every spoonful.

1 Heat a saucepot over medium heat and cook the diced bacon until crisp and light golden brown, 4 to 5 minutes. Use a slotted spoon to remove the bacon for later use. Drain all but 1 Tbsp (15 mL) of the drippings from the pot.

2 Add the onion and cook over medium heat until soft and translucent, about 5 minutes. Stir in the garlic and cook for 1 minute more.

3 Drain the white kidney beans in a colander and rinse with cold water. Reserve 1 cup (250 mL) of the beans and add the rest to the pot. Use a vegetable peeler to peel two strips of lemon zest, and add to the pot. Stir in the water and bring to a boil over high heat, then reduce to a gentle simmer to allow the flavors to meld, stirring occasionally, for 20 minutes.

4 Remove from the heat, discard the lemon zest and puree using an immersion blender until smooth. Return the soup to medium heat, then add the reserved beans and the bacon. Halve the lemon, squeeze in the juice and season to taste.

5 Ladle the soup into bowls and top with a sprinkling of parsley.

Notes:

+ For an added garnish, swirl in 1 tsp (5 mL) of your best olive oil and a grind of black pepper. This is the kind of soup that fuels workers after a long shift, and although some people may instinctively want to reach for the salt, the addition of lemon wakes up the flavor without adding the extra sodium.

YIELD:
10-12 SERVINGS

PREP TIME:
15 MINUTES

COOK TIME:
95 MINUTES

Ham & Barley Soup

I like to use a ham hock to infuse rich flavors into both broth and barley. A single hock will provide enough meat for a large batch of soup, but don't hesitate to do the same with the leftovers from a whole ham dinner.

---

1   Heat the oil in a large soup pot over medium heat and add the onions, celery and carrots. Cook, stirring occasionally, until the onions are translucent, about 5 minutes. Stir in the barley, garlic, thyme, bay leaves and celery salt, and stir for 1 minute more. Drop in the ham hock and add 4 cups (1 L) of the stock and the tomatoes. Loosely cover the pot and bring up to a full simmer. Reduce the heat to medium-low to achieve a gentle simmer, and continue to cook until the barley is tender and the ham hock yields easily when pierced with a fork, about 90 minutes.

2   Remove the ham hock to a cutting board and let cool for 15 minutes. Peel away the skin and trim the meat from the bone, dicing it into bite-sized pieces. Add the ham back to the pot, add the remaining 2 cups (500 mL) of stock, return to a simmer and season to taste.

3   To serve, ladle the soup into bowls and top with the parsley.

2 Tbsp (30 mL) vegetable oil

2 medium onions, diced

2 stalks celery, diced

2 medium carrots, peeled and diced

1 cup (250 mL) pearl barley

2 cloves garlic, minced

2 tsp (10 mL) chopped fresh thyme

2 bay leaves

1 tsp (5 mL) celery salt

1 smoked ham hock (about 2¼ lb/1 kg) or 2 cups (500 mL) diced ham

6 cups (1.5 L) chicken stock or water, divided

1 can (28 oz/796 mL) diced tomatoes

Salt and pepper

Chopped fresh Italian parsley, for garnish

61

Notes:

+   This is one of those dishes that gets better after a day. Don't worry if it looks too thick on the second heating—just add a little water to thin it out.

YIELD: MAKES ONE
10-INCH (25 CM)
PANCAKE

PREP TIME:
10 MINUTES

COOK TIME:
12 MINUTES

Bacon Okonomiyaki

Japanese Cabbage Pancake

1 cup (250 mL) all-purpose
   flour

1 tsp (5 mL) granulated
   sugar

1 tsp (5 mL) baking powder

½ tsp (2 mL) table salt

2 large eggs

2 Tbsp (30 mL) lager beer

2 cups (500 mL) freshly
   grated green cabbage

1 Tbsp (15 mL) canola oil

4 slices bacon, cooked,
   drained and chopped

Okonomi sauce and mayon-
   naise (I like Kewpie
   brand), for serving
   (see note)

Okonomiyaki is an inexpensive snack served in beer joints across
Japan. It's a cabbage pancake cooked on a griddle with whatever
toppings you wish and then brushed with a sweet sauce and mayonnaise. The traditionalists top it with *hana katsuo* (dried tuna
flakes), so go for that if you want the real deal. The basic batter is
easily modified with any topping or garnish you have, and one of
these can be cut up into a couple dozen pieces, so it makes appetizers an easy task.

---

1   Stir together the flour, sugar, baking powder and salt in a large
    mixing bowl. Add 1 cup (250 mL) water, the eggs and beer, and
    whisk until well-blended. Stir in the grated cabbage.

2   Heat the oil in a 10-inch (25 cm) nonstick pan over medium heat.
    Pour in the batter. After 1 minute, give the pan a quick shake to
    loosen the pancake from the bottom. Cook the pancake until the
    bottom starts to get golden (check this by using a spatula to lift it
    up a little) and the pancake begins to rise and firm up around the
    outside edge, 4 to 6 minutes.

3   Arrange the bacon pieces on top of the pancake in a single layer.
    To flip the pancake, slide it out of the pan onto a dinner plate (1)
    and then invert the hot pan over the pancake plate, and in one
    motion, flip the entire plate and the pan back over, so that the pan
    is on the bottom (2). Lift away the plate and continue to cook until
    golden and firm (the bacon side is now at the bottom and will crisp
    up), another 4 to 6 minutes. Using the plate-flipping method again,
    flip the pancake over once more, to make sure the bacon and
    pancake are cooked (3). Insert a skewer or paring knife into the
    center of the pancake. If the skewer comes out clean, it is done.
    Slide the pancake out of the pan and onto a cutting board or platter.

4   To serve, brush the bacon side with the okonomi sauce, then drizzle
    the mayonnaise overtop in a crisscross pattern. Cut the pancake
    into 24 squares and eat while hot.

1.

2.

3.

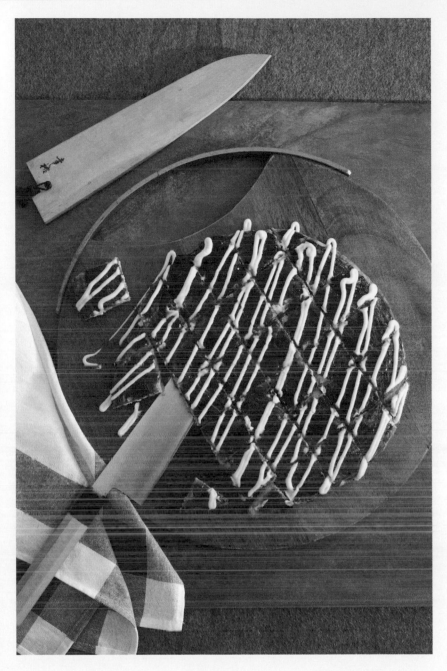

Notes:

+ I make this right in front of my guests after they've arrived—it takes no time and is best right out of the pan.

+ Okonomi sauce can be found in Asian grocery stores, or you can use ⅓ cup (80 mL) ketchup mixed with 2 Tbsp (30 mL) each soy sauce and Worcestershire sauce.

Grilled Kielbasa in Yellow BBQ Sauce

Kielbasa is almost always served cold, but when you talk to the butchers who make it, you'll hear that it is best served hot right out of the smoker oven—they mention this in a quiet voice like it's a secret that can't get out. This recipe can be added to a mixed grill or used as a passed appetizer.

2 Tbsp (30 mL) packed light brown sugar

2 Tbsp (30 mL) white vinegar

2 Tbsp (30 mL) yellow (hot dog) mustard

1 lb (450 g) kielbasa, casing removed

THE DELI COUNTER

1   Preheat the grill to medium.

2   Whisk the brown sugar, vinegar and mustard to combine.

3   Make a series of cuts in the kielbasa in a diamond pattern. These will swell out as it heats and eventually absorb the barbecue glaze. Grill the kielbasa with the lid closed until golden brown, 5 to 8 minutes, turning often. Baste the kielbasa with a coating of the glaze a little at a time as you grill for another 5 to 8 minutes, until the kielbasa reaches an internal temperature of 150°F (65°C).

4   To serve, slice the kielbasa into discs and serve with toothpicks and the remaining sauce for dipping.

Notes:

+   Kielbasa is one of those items I like to get from small, independent butchers, as each one often has their own signature twist on how they make it.

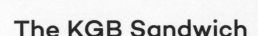

The KGB Sandwich

66

ONION SALAD

½ large white onion, sliced in thin rings

¼ cup (60 mL) white vinegar

2 Tbsp (30 mL) granulated sugar

SANDWICH

4 crusty rolls

½ cup (125 mL) cream cheese

16 slices English cucumber

¾ lb (340 g) garlic salami

½ cup (125 mL) Onion Salad

4 garlic dill pickles, for serving

This is not a delicate tea sandwich, but if you are doing yardwork or something that needs a handful of food to tame a hangry beast, this is your secret weapon. I once made this sandwich for a friend and told him that due to the intense onion and garlic flavor, originally the KGB were the only ones who could handle it.

1 For the onion salad, stir the onion with the vinegar and sugar, and chill in an airtight container (so your fridge won't smell like onions) for at least 30 minutes. This can be prepared and chilled up to 3 days ahead.

2 To make the sandwiches, halve the rolls and spread each half with cream cheese. Lay cucumber slices on the bottom half of each roll. Separate the salami slices and place overtop of the cucumbers. Top the salami with 2 Tbsp (30 mL) of onion salad, cover with the top of the roll and press down firmly. Repeat with the remaining rolls.

3 To serve, cut the sandwich in half and dish up with a garlic dill pickle.

Notes:

+ Choose a good-quality salami from your deli (ask for a taste first) and get it sliced thinly. I like the drier style of salami for this sandwich.

The Five Minute Miracle Sandwich

Cold Cuts to Feed a Crowd

My nephew Curtis used to play in a band called Five Minute Miracle, and once every few months, the van would roll up in front of our house on another cross-country tour. They would emerge from the smelly Chevy exhausted and starving. We would feed the guys before they got back on the road, and I once made the five of them a sandwich so big that it took them 24 hours to finish it—they ate it from Niagara to the western border of Ontario. This version isn't quite as big but only takes about 5 minutes to assemble.

1 large flat round country loaf, halved horizontally

2 Tbsp (30 mL) olive oil

1 tsp (5 mL) dried oregano

1 cup (250 mL) giardiniera (pickled vegetable and olive salad)

150 g (5 oz) sliced ham

150 g (5 oz) sliced salami

150 g (5 oz) sliced capicola

150 g (5 oz) sliced provolone or Swiss cheese

½ cup (125 mL) roasted red bell peppers

½ cup (125 mL) Onion Salad (page 66)

2 cups (500 mL) arugula, washed and trimmed

8 stuffed green olives

1   Open up the country loaf and have all of the ingredients close at hand. If the bread is very thick, remove some of the inside with your hands. Brush each cut side of the loaf with the olive oil and sprinkle with the oregano.

2   Drain the giardiniera and either chop by hand or pulse in a food processor. Spread a single layer of the giardiniera on each half of the bread. Layer on half of the ham, salami and capicola, followed by the cheese, bell peppers, onion salad and arugula. Repeat this layering process with the remaining ingredients. Put the top half of the country loaf on and wrap tightly with plastic wrap. Place the sandwich between two plates and wrap tightly with plastic again to press the sandwich together. Refrigerate for at least 1 hour.

3   To serve, unwrap and cut into 8 wedges, each held together with a large toothpick stuck through an olive.

Notes:

+ This sandwich was inspired by a muffuletta I tasted in New Orleans, but we have taken our own version down the road here. If you can't find giardiniera, use a pickled vegetable mix—it's all about the sour.

Canucklehead Sandwich

with Peameal Bacon, Cheddar, Maple Mustard & Pickles

70

LIVING HIGH OFF THE HOG

1 Tbsp (15 mL) butter

12 slices (about 300 g)
peameal bacon

4 large kaiser rolls

3 Tbsp (45 mL) grainy
mustard

1 Tbsp (15 mL) pure maple
syrup

½ cup (125 mL) coarsely
grated old white
cheddar

½ cup (125 mL) sliced
bread and butter
pickles

Peameal bacon is a sweet, pickled pork loin that is an Ontario classic. Chances are that if you show up to a community event like a farmers' market or pond hockey tournament (yes, The Hip will be on the stereo), it will be on the menu. She's a beauty, eh?

─────────

1   Melt the butter in a skillet over medium-high heat and fry the peameal bacon for 3 minutes per side.

2   To assemble, halve the kaiser rolls horizontally. Stir together the mustard and maple syrup, then spread the mixture on the inside of the kaiser rolls, top and bottom. Layer the peameal bacon slices on the bottom of each roll, and top with the cheese and pickles.

3   The sandwiches can be served immediately or wrapped in foil or parchment and warmed in a 300°F (150°C) oven for 10 minutes to melt the cheese.

Notes:

+   Peameal is most often sliced and fried, but if you're cooking for a crowd, you can roast the whole piece to an internal

temperature of 165°F (74°C) and carve it into thin slices. If you can't find peameal, use ham made from pork loin or even leftover roast pork.

YIELD: 6-8 SERVINGS
AS AN APPETIZER

PREP TIME:
10 MINUTES

COOK TIME:
60 MINUTES

Kielbasa Orloff Wellington

My wife, Anna, and I both studied culinary arts and had to memorize and recreate classical European dishes like veal Orloff with caramelized onions, and beef Wellington, which is baked in pastry. Inspired by those classics, I have taken good old kielbasa and fancied it up with some technique. Put on your Canadian tuxedo and raise that pinky finger. This dish can be sliced and served as a passed appetizer or on a brunch buffet.

---

1   Preheat the oven to 400°F (200°C) and line a baking sheet with parchment paper.

2   Cook the onions in the vegetable oil over medium heat until soft and golden brown, about 35 minutes. Add the thyme, deglaze with the brandy and set aside to cool (this can be done ahead of time).

3   Peel away the outer casing from the kielbasa and make a series of slices halfway into the kielbasa every ¾ inch (2 cm) from the inside of the curve. Flatten the kielbasa onto the cutting board to open up the slices, then stuff each slice with the onion mixture.

4   Lay the thawed puff pastry sheet on the prepared tray and spread the mustard in a line across the middle. Place the kielbasa overtop the mustard. Brush the edges of the puff pastry with the egg wash, then roll up to encase the kielbasa. Seal the edges and turn the pastry over so the seam is on the bottom. Brush with the egg wash, sprinkle with poppy seeds and bake in the preheated oven until golden brown, 20 to 25 minutes.

2 medium onions, sliced

1 Tbsp (15 mL) vegetable oil

1 tsp (5 mL) chopped fresh thyme

1 oz (30 mL) brandy

1 lb (450 g) smoked kielbasa

1 sheet (8 oz/225 g) frozen butter puff pastry, thawed in the fridge

2 Tbsp (30 mL) grainy mustard

1 lightly whisked large egg + 2 Tbsp (30 mL) water, for brushing

1 Tbsp poppy seeds

Notes:

+   To get ahead, wrap the kielbasa and onions in the puff pastry and chill until ready to cook, then take it right from the fridge to the oven and bake until golden brown and crisp.

Spaghetti Carbonara

1 lb (450 g) dry spaghetti

1 Tbsp (15 mL) olive oil

5 oz (150 g) diced pancetta (about ½ cup/125 mL)

1 clove garlic, minced

1 tsp (5 mL) ground black pepper, plus extra for serving

3 large eggs

½ cup (125 mL) grated pecorino Romano cheese, plus extra for serving

Salt

In Italy, there are some pasta dishes that are such classics, you would never dare change anything about them. I used to look to this dish after long shifts in the kitchen because I could make a meal out of a handful of simple ingredients that left me satisfied and with only a few dishes to clean up. Named after coal miners, it is rich from the egg and cheese but spiked with bacon, garlic and black pepper—I like to add lots of extra pepper on top.

1 Boil the pasta in a large pot of salted water over high heat according to the package directions. Ladle out ½ cup (125 mL) of the pasta water before draining the pasta in a colander.

2 While the pasta is boiling, heat the olive oil in a large sauté pan over medium heat and add the pancetta, stirring and cooking until crisp, about 6 minutes. Stir in the garlic and pepper.

3 Whisk the eggs and cheese in a small bowl and set aside. Add the reserved pasta water to the pancetta and increase the heat to medium-high to warm through. Add the pasta and toss it with tongs to coat it with the sauce and warm it through. Remove the pan from the heat. Add the egg and cheese mixture, tossing the pasta until it's fully coated (the warm pasta will heat the eggs through and melt the cheese). Season to taste—it may not need added salt, depending on the pancetta.

4 Serve immediately with extra cheese and black pepper sprinkled on top.

Notes:

+ Follow the recommended cooking time on dry pasta packaging. I've cooked for decades and find the package is always accurate.

The last time I made this, the cooking time on the spaghetti was 11½ minutes, and yes, that half-minute was important.

Fettuccine all'Amatriciana

When you watch someone who is really good at what they do, you notice that they make great things without making them complicated. I recall watching two chef friends (Claudio and Mario) prepare this dish for a large group. I snuck a bowl with them in the back kitchen, sitting on milk crates, eating like kings. This dish is simple and delicious—noodles in a bacon, tomato and cheese sauce. And it goes nicely with a glass of Chianti!

1 lb (450 g) dry fettuccine

4 oz (120 g) guanciale, julienned

3 cups (750 mL) tomato sauce

½ cup (125 mL) dry white wine

1 tsp (5 mL) dried chili flakes

Salt and pepper

2 Tbsp (30 mL) olive oil

½ cup (125 mL) grated pecorino cheese

77

THE DELI COUNTER

1   Boil the pasta in a large pot of salted water over high heat according to the package directions. Ladle out ½ cup (125 mL) of the pasta water before draining the pasta in a colander.

2   While the pasta is cooking, cook the guanciale in a large sauté pan over medium heat until it loses its pink color and curls up, about 5 minutes. Stir in the tomato sauce, wine and chili flakes, and bring to a full simmer, still over medium heat.

3   Return the pasta to the pot, season with salt and pepper, and toss with the olive oil and reserved pasta water. Add the cheese to the pasta and mix well to coat. Serve the pasta in bowls and top with the sauce.

Notes:

+   If you make your own sauce, great. I actually use a brand called Marinelli's, which is locally made in Niagara, but available at Sobey's. If you can find a tomato sauce that is not sweet and has excellent tomato flavor, it's a good staple to keep in the pantry.

YIELD: 6 SERVINGS
MAKES ONE 12-INCH
(2.5 L) CASSEROLE

PREP TIME:
15 MINUTES

COOK TIME:
1 HOUR 45 MINUTES

Choucroute

Sauerkraut Baked with Sausages

1 Tbsp (15 mL) vegetable oil

1 medium onion, chopped

2 medium Yukon Gold potatoes, peeled and cut in ½-inch (1 cm) dice

3 sprigs fresh thyme

1 bay leaf

1 can (28 oz/796 mL) sauerkraut, drained but not rinsed

½ lb (225 g) pork wieners

½ lb (225 g) kielbasa

½ lb (225 g) smoked sausages

¼ lb (115 g) double-smoked bacon

2 cups (500 mL) lager beer

Years ago, we traveled to the Alsace area of France to visit the wine region and dine on the local specialties. This was an important learning opportunity, as I realized that sauerkraut is not used as a condiment there (like I had always seen back home) but rather as a vegetable. I kept seeing elegant people place heaping piles of sauerkraut on pork sausages for lunch, and we now look to this as a go-to dinner when the first cold weather comes to us every autumn.

1 Preheat the oven to 325°F (160°C).

2 Heat the oil in a medium sauté pan over medium heat and add the onion and potatoes. Sauté until the onion softens, 5 to 8 minutes. Stir in the thyme sprigs and bay leaf, then remove the pan from the heat. Stir the sauerkraut in with the onion mixture and then spread it into a 12-inch (2.5 L) baking dish or casserole.

3 Score the wieners lengthwise, making slices just into the surface of the skin (this will allow them to swell and absorb the sauerkraut flavor), and cut each into 4 pieces. Remove the outer casing of the kielbasa and cut into ½-inch (1 cm) thick slices. Split the smoked sausages in half lengthwise and score through the casing to make a diamond pattern. Remove the tough skin from the double-smoked bacon, if using slab, and cut the bacon into bite-sized pieces. Arrange all of the cut meats on top of the sauerkraut, pressing in gently, then pour in the beer. Cover the dish with a lid or foil and bake for 1 hour, then uncover and cook until the meat is piping hot throughout (175°F/80°C) and the potatoes are tender, about 30 minutes more.

4 Serve with a variety of mustards (I like sweet, grainy and hot), sour cream (if desired) and buttered rye bread.

Notes:

+ When you go to buy sauerkraut, be a big shot and get the most expensive— your family deserves it, and it only costs a dollar more than the cheap stuff. Look for fermented sauerkraut, not one that has just been pickled in vinegar, as the taste is milder and always more satisfying.

GROUND AND DICED

OLSON HARDWARE

MODEL: 410 **MANUFACTURER:** Hobart **YEAR:** 1940

NOTES: Referred to as "the streamliner," this slicer, designed by Egmont Arens, reflects modernist style lines with curves like an airplane's wing. An example is displayed at the Museum of Modern Art in New York City.

YIELD: 16 SERVINGS
MAKES ONE 8 ½ X
4 ½-INCH (1.3 L) LOAF
PAN OR TERRINE

PREP TIME:
40 MINUTES

COOK TIME:
90 MINUTES

Country Terrine

with Grand Marnier Prunes, Pecans & Prosciutto

Traditionally, a terrine is the earthenware dish a meat pie is cooked in and served from. This recipe can be done in a special terrine dish or a smaller metal loaf tin—at the end of the day, it is simply a fancy meatloaf. It makes a great starter for a multicourse meal, as all the work is done ahead of time and you only have to slice and plate it. It looks and tastes like a million bucks, with its wrapping of pink ham and mosaic of nuts and dried fruits inside.

1 Preheat the oven to 325°F (160°C).

2 Pour the milk over the diced bread and stir in the mustard. Let the mixture sit in the fridge until the bread is soft and can be stirred into a paste using a spoon, about 20 minutes. (This mixture is called a panada and will hold the terrine together and absorb any meat juices that would otherwise leak into the pan. See page 23 for more information on panadas.)

3 In a separate bowl, sprinkle the Grand Marnier over the dried apples, prunes and pecans. Cover and let sit for 15 minutes on the counter so the fruit can absorb the liqueur.

4 Lightly grease a loaf pan and measure enough parchment paper so it hangs over the sides. (This parchment will be lined with a layer of prosciutto that will wrap around the terrine to keep it moist and add a sweet, salty flavor.) Lay the parchment paper flat on the work surface and place the prosciutto slices, slightly overlapping, on the parchment paper, reserving 2 or 3 prosciutto slices. Carefully place the prosciutto-lined parchment paper in the pan, with the prosciutto layer facing up.

5 Stir the salt, pepper and allspice into the ground pork, then stir in the panada and the dried fruit mixture, being sure to mix thoroughly to spread the solids and seasonings throughout the ground meat.

1 cup (250 mL) 2% milk

4 slices sandwich bread, crusts removed and diced (about 2 cups/500 mL)

2 Tbsp (30 mL) grainy mustard

¼ cup (60 mL) Grand Marnier or apple juice

½ cup (125 mL) chopped dried apple slices

½ cup (125 mL) chopped pitted prunes

½ cup (125 mL) pecan halves

¼ lb (115 g) thinly sliced prosciutto (about 10 slices)

4 tsp (20 mL) coarse salt

1 tsp (5 mL) ground black pepper

½ tsp (2 mL) ground allspice

2¼ lb (1 kg) ground pork

CONTINUES

6   Using a spoon, pack the ground meat mixture into the prosciutto-lined pan, forcing it into the corners and pressing down to avoid any air bubbles. Lay the remaining slices of prosciutto on top so the terrine is entirely lined. Fold the overhanging parchment over to cover the top. If you are using a terrine with a lid, place it on top; otherwise, cover the loaf pan tightly with foil. Place the terrine in a large roasting pan and pour boiling hot water into the pan until it comes halfway up the side of the terrine—this will keep the temperature constant and prevent browning on the sides. Carefully transfer the roasting pan and terrine to the oven and bake (with the roasting pan uncovered) until the terrine reaches an internal temperature of 165°F (74°C), about 1½ hours. Carefully transfer the terrine from the roasting pan to a rack to cool to room temperature, then refrigerate overnight before slicing.

7   To serve, cut the terrine into slices and plate with a mustard, chutney or pickle mix; a few lettuce leaves; and crusty bread or toast points. The flavor of this terrine will improve if it sits in the fridge for 2 days, and it can be kept for up to 5 days. It can be tightly wrapped and frozen for up to 3 months, then thawed in the fridge for 1 day.

Notes:

+   If you use a standard loaf pan instead of the terrine form, your cook time might have to be adjusted. Use your meat thermometer to confirm an internal temperature of 165°F (74°C). You can switch up the types of dried fruit and nuts to change the color and flavor—try apricots, cherries, cranberries, pistachios or walnuts. Once you get comfortable with the technique, you will be able to get creative with the garnish.

YIELD: 12–16 SERVINGS
MAKES ONE 9-INCH
(23 CM) PIE

PREP TIME:
40 MINUTES

COOK TIME:
2 HOURS 45 MINUTES,
PLUS RESTING

Pork-a-Leekie Pie

This is a showstopper to feed a crowd, and I actually like it even better served cold the next day with pickles or relish, like a ploughman's lunch. It's true that this is a complex recipe, but you can plan to make it well ahead of time, and much of the cooking can happen in the same pot. The amount of work you put into getting it prepared will be rewarded by the ease of satisfying cravings once the pie is done.

2 leeks

1 (800 g) smoked ham hock (see note)

1 lb (450 g) ground pork

1 tsp (5 mL) coarse salt

1 tsp (5 mL) ground black pepper

¼ tsp (1 mL) ground cloves

¼ tsp (1 mL) ground cardamom

2 large eggs

1 cup (250 mL) dry bread crumbs

1 recipe Anna's Pie Dough, shaped into a disc and chilled (recipe follows)

6 hard-boiled large eggs, peeled

1 lightly whisked large egg + 2 Tbsp (30 mL) water, for brushing

85

1 Trim off the tops of the leeks and cut each leek in half so the white and green parts are separate. Wash the green parts of the leeks and place them in a soup pot. Dice the white parts of the leeks, rinse well in a colander and set aside.

2 Place the smoked ham hock in the pot with the leek greens and add 3 cups (750 mL) of water, or enough to cover the ham hock. Bring to a boil, uncovered, over medium-high heat. Then reduce to a simmer over medium heat, cover loosely and cook until a fork pulls out easily, about 1 hour. Remove the ham hock to a dish to cool, and remove and discard the leek greens. Add the white leeks to the stock and simmer over medium heat until they are tender, about 20 minutes.

3 While the white leeks are cooking, remove and discard the skin from the ham hock. Trim away the tender meat and cut it into ½-inch (1 cm) dice. You should end up with about 2 cups (500 mL) of meat. Once the white leeks are tender, use a slotted spoon to transfer them to a bowl and let cool. Let the stock cool to room temperature. Measure out 1 cup (250 mL) of the stock for the pie (the rest can be saved for other uses). This can all be prepared 1 day ahead. Chill the ham hock, cooked white leeks and stock separately.

4 Preheat the oven to 400°F (200°C).

CONTINUES

5 Mix the ground pork with the salt, pepper, cloves and cardamom, and then stir in the 2 eggs, the reserved 1 cup (250 mL) of ham stock and bread crumbs. Add in reserved meat and cooked white leeks and stir to combine well (1). Chill this mixture while rolling the pastry.

6 Remove one-third of the chilled dough and set aside. On a lightly floured surface, roll out the larger piece of dough (the remaining two-thirds) into a circle just under ¼-inch (6 mm) thick; place it into the bottom and up the sides of an ungreased 9-inch (23 cm) springform pan (2). Roll out the remaining dough to a circle of the same thickness for the top of the pie. Cut several large holes from the top piece of dough to allow the steam to escape while baking (3), then place it on a plate and chill while filling the pie.

7 Spoon half of the meat mixture into the pastry-lined pan and spread it out evenly (4,5). Arrange the eggs in a circle (like the numbers on a clock) on top of the meat mixture and gently press in a little (6). Spoon the remaining meat mixture over the eggs, pressing in between to make sure there are no air pockets (7), and spread it so it's level. Place the pastry top directly on the meat pie, sealing the edges with a pinch and trimming any excess dough from the sides (8). Brush the top of the pie with the egg wash (9) and bake for 15 minutes, then reduce the heat to 350°F (180°C) and cook until the center of the pie comes to an internal temperature of 165°F (74°C), 60 to 75 minutes more.

8 Remove the pie and let rest for at least 10 minutes before slicing (10). It is delicious served warm, but I prefer it right out of the fridge. To serve, remove the outer ring of the springform pan and transfer the pie from the pan base to a platter. Slice into portions and serve with pickles, relish or chutney. The pie will keep for 5 days in the fridge. To make ahead and freeze, let it cool overnight, then cut into quarters and wrap tightly—it will keep in the freezer for up to 2 months.

Notes:

+ Choose condiments with high notes of sweet and sour, like honey mustard and dill pickles, or potato salad and pickled beets.

+ Be sure to purchase a *ham* hock (smoked and cooked), not a fresh pork hock, in order to get the smoky ham character and full, rich flavor in the stock.

YIELD: MAKES
ENOUGH FOR A
DOUBLE-CRUST PIE

PREP TIME:
10 MINUTES,
PLUS CHILLING

COOK TIME: NONE

Anna's Pie Dough

This is the dough my wife uses for fruit pies, but the flaky texture and ease of handling also make it a great choice for savory pastries like the Pork-a-Leekie (page 85). Anna knows me too well—I'm impatient, but this dough is hard to mess up. You don't have to worry about the butter being ice-cold, plus pulling the dough out of the fridge 30 minutes before rolling makes it easier to handle.

1 Combine the flour, sugar and salt in a bowl. Add the oil and blend in using a pastry cutter, electric beaters or a stand mixer fitted with the paddle attachment, until the flour looks evenly crumbly in texture.

2 Add the butter and cut in until rough and crumbly but small pieces of butter are still visible. Stir the water and vinegar together and add all at once to the flour mixture, mixing just until the dough comes together. Shape the dough into a disc, wrap in plastic and chill until firm, at least 1 hour. The dough can be made up to 2 days ahead and stored chilled, or it can be frozen for up to 3 months and thawed in the fridge before rolling.

2½ cups (625 mL) all-purpose flour

1 Tbsp (15 mL) granulated sugar

1 tsp (5 g) fine salt

3 Tbsp (45 mL) vegetable oil

1 cup (225 g) cool unsalted butter, cut into pieces

¼ cup (60 mL) cool water

2 tsp (10 mL) white vinegar or lemon juice

89

GROUND AND JICED

Notes:

+ A good pie dough is a staple for serious home cooks, and this one is the best. The addition of a little oil to the flour before adding in the butter prevents the flour from absorbing too much water, leaving the pastry flaky and tender.

YIELD: 12 SERVINGS
MAKES 2 CUPS
(500 ML)

PREP TIME:
20 MINUTES

COOK TIME:
3 HOURS

Pork Rillettes

LIVING HIGH OFF THE HOG

1½ lb (675 g) diced pork
   shoulder, including fat

2 Tbsp (30 mL) diced onion

1 tsp (5 mL) coarse salt

½ tsp (2 mL) ground
   cloves

½ tsp (2 mL) ground
   allspice

½ tsp (2 mL) chopped
   fresh thyme

This dish is from the same family as pâté—a delicious, rich and highly flavored meat spread for snacks or starters. The benefit of it being in a jar is that you can easily dig it out with a knife and slather it on bread. It's not smooth like butter but rather like shredded juicy meat, and the spices make me think of a holiday meal. It's so easy to pull out a jar when guests stop by (or maybe after they leave).

1 Preheat the oven to 325°F (160°C).

2 Spread the diced pork shoulder in single layer in a small roasting pan and cook, uncovered, until the fat has rendered out and the meat is a dark brown color, about 2½ hours.

3 Stir in the onion, salt, cloves, allspice and thyme, and cook until the onions are soft, about 30 minutes more. Cool the pan on a rack to room temperature.

4 Transfer the meat mixture, including the drippings, to a food processor and pulse to a spreadable texture. Spoon the rillettes into ramekins or small jars, cover and refrigerate.

5 To serve, put out the rillettes with toast points, mustard and pickles. A small knife can be used to spread the rillettes onto the toasts. This is a nice welcome as a starter with a glass of sparkling wine and sets the pace for a terrific meal. The rillettes will keep for 1 week in the fridge.

Notes:

+ Don't be tempted to discard
   the drippings from the
   pan—they're what keep the
   meat moist and spreadable.

Rillettes can also be made
with rabbit, duck or even
salmon. This goes back to a
pre-refrigeration way of
preserving meat.

Sausage Stuffed Jalapeño Peppers

with Lime Crema

Stuffed jalapeños are often on my menu for get-togethers with friends, whether outside around the grill or hot-from-the-oven inside. These two-bite appetizers are packed with a juicy sausage-cheese filling and glazed with just a kiss of sweet BBQ sauce.

1   Preheat the oven to 350°F (180°C), and line a baking sheet with parchment paper.

2   Wash the jalapeño peppers, cut in half lengthwise, and use a teaspoon to remove the seeds and membrane. You can leave the stems or cut them off.

3   Stir together the sausage, eggs, bread crumbs and cheese until well-combined. Stuff each of the jalapeño halves with the sausage mix, packing it in well. Lay the stuffed peppers on the prepared tray and bake until brown and puffy, about 15 minutes.

4   While the peppers are baking, stir together the BBQ sauce and vinegar. Brush it on the tops of the stuffed jalapeños after the initial 15 minutes cooking time. Cook to set the glaze and reach an internal temperature of 165°F (74°C), another 3 to 5 minutes.

5   For the lime crema, stir together the sour cream, lime juice and cilantro, and season to taste.

6   To serve, arrange the stuffed peppers on a tray with the lime crema in a side dish. Spoon some of the crema on a pepper and chomp away. These can be assembled up to 1 day in ahead and kept covered in the fridge until ready to bake.

12 fresh jalapeño peppers

1 lb (450 g) honey garlic or mild Italian sausages), casings removed

2 large eggs

½ cup (125 mL) dry bread crumbs

½ cup (125 mL) grated Parmigiano-Reggiano cheese

¼ cup (60 mL) BBQ sauce

2 Tbsp (30 mL) white vinegar

1 cup (250 mL) sour cream

2 Tbsp (30 mL) fresh lime juice

1 Tbsp (15 mL) chopped fresh cilantro

Salt

93

GROUND AND DICED

Notes:

+   The finishing BBQ glaze makes these morsels shiny and adds a nice, smoky character. You can choose different BBQ sauces to your own liking to switch things up. Keep in mind, too, that jalapeños might all look similar, but the heat levels can vary, so taste before you make these and use your judgment to find ones suitable to the preferred heat level of your crowd. They should have a balance of great flavor with a little kick, but not be so hot that every bite brings tears to your eyes.

YIELD: 10-12
SERVINGS
MAKES 48 PIECES

PREP TIME:
10 MINUTES

COOK TIME:
15 MINUTES

When Pigs Fly

Spicy Grilled Pork Nibbles

This grilled finger food is a nice pass-around starter, or it can be added to a salad for an easy lunch. The original inspiration is a Filipino version of bacon called *tocino*, which is cured overnight with lots of sugar and then fried to go with breakfast. This recipe is marinated with a barbecue rub and done on the grill, and enjoyed as a snack just like chicken wings (hence the name). I love the crispy brown bits on barbecued foods—these snacks are basically all that good stuff: sticky, slightly charred, spicy and sweet. It's impossible to eat just one.

2 lb (900 g) boneless loin

¼ cup (60 mL) Basic BBQ Rub (page 267)

2 Tbsp (30 mL) dried chili flakes

Juice of 2 limes

Your Favorite Blue Cheese Dip, for serving (recipe follows)

1　Remove any extra fat and the silver skin from the loin (see page 21 for tips), and cut the meat into ⅛-inch (3 mm) thin slices—each piece should be 1 to 2 bites.

2　Stir the meat with the BBQ rub, chili flakes and lime juice, thoroughly massaging it in with your hands to get complete coverage. Cover and refrigerate for 1 hour to allow the marinade to penetrate the meat.

3　Heat the grill to 350°F (180°C) and cook for 4 minutes per side. Test a piece by cutting in half—it should be cooked but still juicy. Serve with blue cheese dip.

Notes:

+ The amount of dried chili flakes can be adjusted to the taste of your guests.

Your Favorite Blue Cheese Dip

1 cup (250 mL) mayonnaise

½ cup (125 mL) sour cream

½ cup (125 mL) crumbled
blue cheese

1 tsp (5 mL) garlic powder

2 Tbsp (30 mL) thinly
sliced green onions

3 dashes Worcestershire
sauce

3 dashes hot sauce
(optional)

LIVING HIGH OFF THE HOG

96

1   Stir together the mayonnaise, sour cream, blue cheese and garlic
powder, breaking down the blue cheese pieces as you combine.
Stir in the green onions, Worcestershire and hot sauce (if using),
and chill until ready to serve. The dip will keep, refrigerated, for up
to 5 days.

Notes:

+   Celery and carrot sticks
are an easy add-on and also
wonderful with the blue

cheese dip. Any leftovers
will make an amazing sandwich with the blue cheese
as a spread.

Ranch Dressing

Ranch is such a common grocery item that you may never have thought to make your own—it's cool, creamy and quite low in fat. It can be used as a dressing for greens, a dip for appetizers or even as a spread for sandwiches using leftover roast, BBQ or meatloaf.

---

1 Whisk all of the ingredients together and season to taste with salt and lots of pepper. Keep covered in the fridge for up to 5 days.

½ cup (125 mL) buttermilk

3 Tbsp (45 mL) Greek yogurt (0% MF is fine)

3 Tbsp (45 mL) mayonnaise

2 green onions, finely chopped

¾ tsp (4 mL) garlic powder

Salt and pepper

GROUND AND DICED

Notes:

+ This sauce is also fantastic on Sausage Burgers (page 131) or sandwiches made out of crispy Pork Schnitzel (page 179). It can also be made with fresh garlic, but the powder has a certain recognizable flavor that works well in this application.

Sausage Stuffed Mushroom Caps

with Ranch Dressing

Mushroom caps make a great little cup for this cheesy sausage bite, perfect as a pass-around appetizer for when your dinner guests arrive. And the ranch dip offers a cool garlic refresher—it's almost like an "anti–breath mint."

---

1   Preheat the oven to 350°F (180°C) and line a baking sheet with parchment paper.

2   Combine the sausage with ½ cup (125 mL) of the panko, along with the cream cheese, lemon juice, chives, mustard and celery salt. Use a small spoon to fill each of the mushrooms with the stuffing, pressing in firmly. Arrange the stuffed mushroom caps on the prepared tray and cover each with a pinch of the remaining ¼ cup (60 mL) of panko. Bake until the panko on top is golden, 20 to 25 minutes.

3   Let the mushrooms cool for 5 minutes, then serve with sides of hot sauce and ranch dressing.

10 oz (280 g) hot Italian sausage meat

¾ cup (175 mL) panko bread crumbs, divided

½ cup (125 mL) cream cheese, at room temperature

2 Tbsp (30 mL) fresh lemon juice

1 Tbsp (15 mL) chopped fresh chives

1 tsp (5 mL) Dijon mustard

½ tsp (2 mL) celery salt

24 medium button mushroom caps, stems removed

Ranch Dressing (page 97)

99

GROUND AND DICED

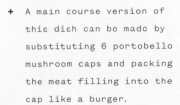

Notes:

+ A main course version of this dish can be made by substituting 6 portobello mushroom caps and packing the meat filling into the cap like a burger.

YIELD: MAKES 24

PREP TIME:
10 MINUTES,
PLUS CHILLING

COOK TIME:
20 MINUTES

Sausage Rolls

with Dill Pickle & Mozzarella

¾ lb (340 g) ground pork

⅔ cup (160 mL) dry bread crumbs

⅓ cup (80 mL) dill pickle relish or diced dill pickles

1 tsp (5 mL) table salt

1 tsp (5 mL) ground black pepper

3 or 4 dashes Worcestershire sauce

1 sheet (8 oz/225 g) frozen butter puff pastry, thawed in the fridge

3 oz (90 g) mozzarella, cut in sticks

1 lightly whisked large egg + 2 Tbsp (30 mL) water, for brushing

1 Tbsp (15 mL) sesame seeds

Sausage rolls are a great make-ahead for snacking or packing into a lunch box. These rolls are special because the recipe has you making your own sausage, so you can control the amount of seasoning to your family's liking. They can be eaten cold or reheated. I recommend serving them with a selection of beer as an official taste test while the big game is on TV. As long as it's official, I'll have just one more.

1   Combine the ground pork with the bread crumbs, relish, salt, pepper and Worcestershire (using your hands is easiest). Chill until ready to assemble.

2   Cut the puff pastry sheet in half. Spoon half of the meat mixture down the center length of 1 pastry sheet, packing it into a cylindrical shape (like a sausage). Repeat with the remaining half of the meat on the remaining pastry sheet. Press the mozzarella into the meat mixture, creating an straight line on each. Brush a long edge of the pastry with the egg wash and roll it over the meat mixture so that it meets the other side of the pastry, and press to seal. Wrap each portion in plastic and chill in the fridge for at least 20 minutes. The rolls can also be assembled up to a day ahead and chilled, or frozen to be thawed in the fridge overnight and baked later.

3   Preheat the oven to 400°F (200°C) and line a baking sheet with parchment paper.

4   Cut each log into 12 pieces and arrange on the prepared tray. Brush the top of each piece with egg wash and sprinkle with sesame seeds. Bake until the pastry is golden brown and the sausage reaches an internal temperature of 165°F (74°C), about 20 minutes.

Notes:

+   Working with the pastry straight from the fridge makes it easy to handle, and chilling the rolls before baking ensures the pastry will puff up, earning its name. For variety, you can use a different cheese in the sausage filling or switch out the dill pickle relish with a spicy chutney.

YIELD: MAKES 24

PREP TIME:
15 MINUTES,
PLUS CHILLING

COOK TIME:
50 MINUTES

Empanadas

Empanadas are little meat-filled turnovers that are eaten all over Latin America, and I've enjoyed a wide variety in our travels to Chile and Argentina. The ones in Mendoza, Argentina, typically use ground beef, but pork easily takes on the spices and olive flavors in this recipe. These "hand pies" are part of an international grouping of portable snacks that include Cornish pasties and Jamaican patties. Typically, restaurant empanadas are deep-fried, but home versions are most often baked in the oven.

---

1 Heat the oil over medium-high heat in a skillet and add the onions. Sauté until the onions start to brown, about 5 minutes, then reduce the heat to medium and continue to cook, stirring occasionally, until soft and golden brown, 10 to 15 minutes. Stir in the pork and salt, and cook until the pork crumbles easily and is no longer pink, 5 to 7 minutes. Stir in the bell pepper, cumin, paprika and oregano, and cook until the bell pepper softens, about 3 minutes. Then add ½ cup (125 mL) of water and continue to cook until the water is absorbed, about 5 minutes more. Remove the pan from the heat and stir in the green onions. Cool the filling to room temperature. Use a box grater to grate the hard-boiled eggs (1) and stir in (2). The filling can be prepared ahead of time and refrigerated until ready to assemble.

CONTINUES

2 Tbsp (30 mL) vegetable oil

2 medium onions, diced (about 2 cups/500 mL)

1 lb (450 g) ground pork

1 tsp (5 mL) table salt

½ seeded and diced red bell pepper (about ½ cup/125 mL)

2 Tbsp (30 mL) ground cumin

1 Tbsp (15 mL) smoked paprika

1 tsp (5 mL) dried oregano

1 cup (250 mL) sliced green onions

4 hard-boiled large eggs, peeled

1 recipe Empanada Dough (recipe follows)

24 pimiento-stuffed olives

1 lightly whisked large egg + 2 Tbsp (30 mL) water, for brushing (if baking)

Chimichurri (page 203), for serving

1.

2.

3.

2   Line a baking sheet with parchment paper. To assemble the empanadas, slice the dough into 24 equal pieces (3, previous page). On a lightly floured surface, roll each piece of dough into a 5-inch (12.5 cm) circle that is about ¼-inch (6 mm) thick, trimming away any rough edges (or use a cookie cutter to trim).

3   To fill each empanada, use a pastry brush dipped in water to lightly moisten half of the outside edge of 1 pastry circle. Spoon in 2 Tbsp (30 mL) of the meat filling, plus 1 olive, and then pinch the sides to seal the pastry into a half-moon shape. For a scalloped seal, pinch the sealed edge by starting at one end and making a series of overlapping little folds (the seal will look like a braided rope). Lay the empanada on the prepared baking sheet. Repeat with the remaining dough and filling. Once all the empanadas have been filled, they can be chilled until ready to cook.

4   To bake the empanadas, preheat the oven to 350°F (180°C). Brush the tops of the empanadas with the egg wash and bake until lightly browned and the pork filling is fully cooked and reaches an internal temperature of 165°F (74°C), about 20 minutes. To deep-fry the empanadas, heat vegetable oil in a tabletop deep fryer to 350°F (180°C) and fry 4 or 5 at a time until golden brown, about 4 minutes. Drain the empanadas on a tray lined with paper towel and keep warm or reheat in a 250°F (120°C) oven.

5   To serve, place the warm empanadas on a platter with cocktail napkins, with hot sauce or chimichurri on the side.

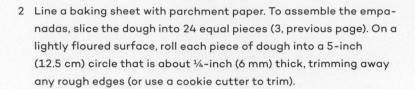

Notes:

+   Filling variations could include BBQ Pulled Pork (page 257), ham and cheese, leftover Pork Sirloin Vindaloo (page 158) or Chili to Celebrate the New Big Screen (page 138).

Empanada Dough

1 Pulse the flour, butter and salt together in a food processor until it looks sandy. Add the warm water and egg, and pulse until the dough comes together into a ball. Shape the dough into a cylinder about 12 inches (30 cm) long, wrap in plastic wrap and chill for at least 2 hours.

3 cups (750 mL) all-purpose flour

½ cup (125 mL) unsalted butter, cut in small pieces, room temperature

½ tsp (2 mL) table salt

¾ cup (175 mL) warm water

1 large egg

GROUND AND DICED

YIELD: 8 SERVINGS
AS AN APPETIZER

PREP TIME:
15 MINUTES

COOK TIME:
10 MINUTES

Pork Satays

with Peanut Dipping Sauce

Satays are Southeast Asian street food snacking skewers, little one- or two-bite delights, while kebabs and skewers are intended as a meal. When we visited Singapore, we capped off our evening with a crawl of one of the many hawker centers, where vendors brag that they've got the best food in town. I like the satays at Lau Pa Sat, an old market building nestled in a block of financial high-rises, with so many charcoal grills pumping out smoky satays that the whole place looks like a foggy, delicious haze.

1   Soak the bamboo skewers in water for at least 1 hour, this will prevent them from scorching on the grill.

2   Cut the pork across the grain into 16 strips, about 2 x 1-inch (5 x 2.5 cm) and ½-inch (1 cm) thick, each weighing about 1 oz (30 g). Toss the pork in a bowl with the ginger, garlic, brown sugar, lime juice, rice wine vinegar, hoisin, chili paste and sesame oil, coating the pork well. Cover and chill for at least 2 hours.

3   For the peanut sauce, blend the peanut butter, sugar, soy sauce, lime juice and garlic with 2 Tbsp (30 mL) water in a small pot. Whisk over low heat until smooth, about 2 minutes. Chill until ready to serve.

4   Thread 1 piece of pork onto each skewer. Preheat the grill to medium-high (350°F/180°C) and fold a 12-inch (30 cm) sheet of foil twice to make a 3-inch (8 cm) strip. Place this on the grill to protect the "handles" of the bamboo skewers, and lay the satays on the grill side by side so the handles are on the foil. Grill until cooked and the juices run clear when the satays are lightly pressed, about 4 minutes per side. Serve immediately with peanut sauce and lime wedges.

SATAYS

16 six-inch (15 cm) bamboo skewers

1 lb (450 g) pork tender-loin, silver skin removed (see page 21)

2 Tbsp (30 mL) finely grated fresh ginger

1 clove garlic, minced

2 Tbsp (30 mL) packed light brown sugar

2 Tbsp (30 mL) fresh lime juice

2 Tbsp (30 mL) rice wine vinegar

2 Tbsp (30 mL) hoisin sauce

1 Tbsp (15 mL) chili paste, such as sambal oelek

Dash sesame oil

PEANUT SAUCE

¼ cup (60 mL) peanut butter

1 Tbsp (15 mL) packed light brown sugar

1 Tbsp (15 mL) soy sauce

1 Tbsp (15 mL) lime juice

1 tsp (5 mL) minced garlic

1 lime, cut in 8 wedges, for serving

GROUND AND DICED

Notes:

+   You can also use tender center-cut loin pieces for satays—they cook so quickly that they stay juicy and are just as easy to eat. Chilled sliced cucumbers with a splash of lime are a nice side dish that work well with the peanut sauce and serve to offset the chili heat if you like adding extra spice.

YIELD: 8 SERVINGS
AS AN APPETIZER

PREP TIME:
25 MINUTES,
PLUS CHILLING

COOK TIME:
20 MINUTES

Polynesian Pork & Pineapple Skewers

16 six-inch (15 cm) bamboo
skewers

1 lb (450 g) boneless pork
loin roast

1 can (20 oz/567 g) pine-
apple chunks, drained

¼ cup (60 mL) beer (lager
or ale)

3 Tbsp (45 mL) soy sauce

1 Tbsp (15 mL) packed
light brown sugar

1 Tbsp (15 mL) hot sauce
(or as desired)

1 tsp (5 mL) finely grated
fresh ginger

1 clove garlic, minced

I seem to remember my mother making me a dish like this one, the cool tang of pineapple set against the savory pork. The idea of fruit with meat in a sweet and salty combination just seemed so exotic and had me dreaming of adventures in far-off places that I'd only seen in movies. This is a time to wear your cheesiest tropical beach shirt and break out the steel guitar island music.

1   Soak bamboo skewers in water for at least 1 hour; this will prevent them from scorching on the grill.

2   Trim the pork of excess fat and remove any silver skin (see page 21 for tips). Cut the loin into 1-inch (2.5 cm) cubes. Toss the pork cubes with the pineapple chunks in a bowl along with the beer, soy sauce, brown sugar, hot sauce, ginger and garlic. Cover and refrigerate for at least 20 minutes or up to 2 hours.

3   Assemble the skewers by threading on 2 pork cubes and 2 pineap-ple chunks, alternating between each. You should wind up with 12 to 16 skewers total. Preheat the grill to medium (300°F/150°C) and fold a 12-inch (30 cm) sheet of foil twice to make a 3-inch (8 cm) strip. Place this on the grill to protect the "handles" of the bamboo skewers, and lay the skewers on the grill side by side so that the handles are all on the foil. Grill until the juices are clear when lightly pressed and the pork registers about 145°F (63°C), about 10 minutes per side. To cook the skewers in the oven, preheat to 350°F (180°C) and place the skewers 1 inch (2.5 cm) apart on a baking sheet lined with parchment paper, baking until the juices run clear, about 20 minutes.

Notes:

+ When I first tried to make these skewers, I used fresh pineapple chunks, and they made the pork a strange, soft texture. Fresh pineapple has a natural enzyme that breaks down tissues and can easily take it too far—this enzyme is knocked out during the canning process, so I prefer canned pineapple when making this recipe. You can bring the leftover marinade to a boil and use it to glaze the skewers toward the end of cooking.

Gyoza

The first place I ever ate gyoza was in Takamatsu, Japan, in 1983, as a wide-eyed 19-year-old Canadian prairie boy over there to play hockey for a year. Every day was filled with fascinating adventures and wild stuff. At first taste, I thought, "Man, those are the best perogies ever!" So I became a chef.

1 Line a baking sheet with parchment paper or plastic wrap, and set aside. Stir together the pork, cabbage, soy sauce, ginger and green onion until well-combined.

2 Place 1 wonton wrapper in your hand and, using a small brush, moisten the edge of one side with a little water to help seal it. Place 1 tsp (5 mL) of the meat mixture in the center of the wrapper (1). Fold the wrapper over so the edges meet at one end and the filling sits flat in your hand. As you bring the edges together, fold 4 or 5 pleats into one side of the dough, then press to seal (2). Line up the prepared gyoza on the prepared baking sheet, pressing each gyoza down to create a flat bottom so the sealed edge is on top (3). Refrigerate, covered with plastic wrap, until ready to use, up to 24 hours (see note). To freeze, place the gyoza (still on the baking sheet and covered with plastic wrap) in the freezer until solid, then transfer to a resealable plastic bag. You can then defrost only as many as you need.

GYOZA
¾ lb (340 g) ground pork

2 cups (500 mL) finely shredded green cabbage

2 Tbsp (30 mL) soy sauce

2 tsp (10 mL) finely grated fresh ginger

1 green onion, thinly sliced

1 pkg (100 pieces) small round wonton wrappers

DIPPING SAUCE
2 Tbsp (30 mL) soy sauce

1 Tbsp (15 mL) rice wine vinegar

1 tsp (5 mL) sesame oil

1 tsp (5 mL) vegetable oil

CONTINUES

1.

2.

3.

3 For the sauce, stir together the soy sauce, rice vinegar and sesame oil, and pour into little dishes for dipping.

4 Heat an oven-safe nonstick skillet with a tight-fitting lid over high heat. Add the oil. Arrange as many dumplings in the skillet as you can fit, leaving a little space between them. Let the dumplings start to sizzle, about 1 minute, then add about 1 cup of water—enough to flood the bottom of the pan and come no more than partway up the gyoza but not submerging them—and cover immediately. The water in the pan will boil and steam the dumplings. Steam over high heat for 6 minutes, then remove the lid, allowing any extra water to evaporate, and the dumplings will start to sizzle again. Cook the gyoza until they can be easily loosened from the pan and have crispy, golden brown bottoms, about 1 minute.

5 Serve the gyoza right away with the dipping sauce.

Notes:

+ If you can't find round wonton wrappers, use a round 3-inch (8 cm) cookie cutter to trim square wrappers into circles. The first few you make may not look polished, but don't worry, they will get better as you go, and you'll improve your folding faster than you think.

+ This recipe makes about 100 gyoza, and they freeze well, if you're cooking for a smaller group of people.

 YIELD: 8 SERVINGS

 PREP TIME:
30 MINUTES,
PLUS CHILLING

 COOK TIME:
20 MINUTES

The Madrid Inverso Sandwich

Inside-Out Hot Hamburger

A trip through the Mercado de la Cebada in Madrid inspired this inside-out triangle sandwich of ground meat with a bread stuffing in the middle. I strolled through this market just after noon on a Saturday, when it normally begins to shut down. Many of the vendors had begun a practice of cooking their fresh seafood and meats to sell off at a discount to get rid of their perishable inventory (the market is not open on Sundays), and they also broke out inexpensive drinks and music—a normally reserved environment had turned into a raging house party! I was drawn to a butcher shop that had a big crowd, where everyone was eating these sandwiches, toasting each other and enjoying life. What a beautiful memory.

2 lb (900 g) ground pork

½ cup (125 mL) dry bread crumbs

1 large egg

1 Tbsp (15 mL) smoked Spanish paprika

1 tsp (5 mL) table salt

1 tsp (5 mL) ground black pepper

FILLING

4 tsp (20 mL) olive oil, divided

½ medium onion, finely diced

Salt

2½ cups (625 mL) diced day-old bread, crusts on

½ cup (125 mL) 2% milk

1 Mix the pork with the bread crumbs, egg, paprika, salt and pepper in a bowl (using your hands is easiest). Cover and chill while preparing the filling.

2 Heat a sauté pan over medium heat and add 2 tsp (10 mL) of the oil. Add the onion and sauté until translucent and soft, about 5 minutes. Set aside to cool to room temperature.

3 Line the bottom and sides of a 9-inch (23 cm) square baking pan with plastic wrap, with enough hanging over the sides to meet in the center when folded over. Stir the cooled onion with the bread and milk—it will hold together when squeezed. Pack half of the meat mixture into the pan, pressing into the corners and making it as flat as possible. Add the bread stuffing mix and press flat and level. Pack in the remaining meat mixture, flatten and then tap the pan down to get rid of any air bubbles. Cover with the plastic wrap and refrigerate for at least 1 hour.

4 To cook, remove the meat from the pan to a cutting board, discard the plastic wrap and cut into 4 equal squares. Then cut each square in half diagonally (like cutting a sandwich).

CONTINUES

5   Heat the remaining 2 tsp (10 mL) of oil in a heavy-bottomed skillet over medium-high heat and drop in the meat triangles. Cook for 8 to 10 minutes (reducing the heat to medium if it browns too much), then flip to cook the other side until the meat reaches an internal temperature of 165°F (74°C), 8 to 10 minutes more.

6   Serve the "sandwiches" on a plate with pickles, mayo, mustard or chutney on the side. You can pick them up to eat with your hands or use a fork and knife, if you prefer.

Notes:

+   You can prepare the meat in a pan and refrigerate overnight to blend the flavors and make it easy to cut the sandwiches. If you want to add an extra-crunchy texture, cover the outside with bread crumbs before cooking.

YIELD: 8 SERVINGS
AS AN APPETIZER

PREP TIME:
10 MINUTES

COOK TIME:
30 MINUTES

Super Mario Meatballs

2 lb (900 g) ground pork

1 cup (250 mL) dry bread
   crumbs

2 large eggs

½ cup (125 mL) grated
   Parmigiano-Reggiano
   cheese

1 Tbsp (15 mL) chopped
   fresh Italian parsley

1 clove garlic, minced

1 tsp (5 mL) table salt

½ tsp (2 mL) ground black
   pepper

3 cups (750 mL) good-
   quality seasoned
   tomato sauce

Meatballs have been a part of most North American homes in one way or another, and my version skips the step of browning them prior to saucing. This eliminates the need for extra fat in the pan and will not create splatter on the stove. You simply shape the meatballs, place into a casserole, then cover with your favorite sauce and cook—it's like *amore*.

---

1 Preheat the oven to 350°F (180°C).

2 Mix together the pork, bread crumbs, eggs, cheese, parsley, garlic, salt and pepper until well-combined (using your hands is best). Use a small ice-cream scoop or spoon to portion 32 meatballs and drop them onto a tray or plate. Round each portion into a ball between your palms.

3 Pour a little tomato sauce into the bottom of an ungreased large casserole dish, spreading it to cover the bottom. Arrange the meatballs on the sauce, leaving just a little space between them. Pour the remaining tomato sauce overtop (the sauce will not submerge the meatballs). Bring to a gentle simmer on the stovetop and then bake, uncovered, until the meatballs are firm and no longer pink in the middle and the internal temperature is 165°F (74°C), about 25 minutes.

4 Serve with toothpicks as a pass-around snack, load into crusty rolls for a sandwich or serve over pasta for a bowl of Italian comfort.

Notes:

+ You can make these meat-balls ahead and freeze in a single layer in resealable plastic bags. Thaw overnight in the fridge and reheat in sauce over moderate heat.

Green Curry Meatballs with Coconut

The flavors of Southeast Asia have become part of the North American palate, and people love Thai curry, whether fiery hot green, aromatic red or mild but still exotic yellow. Decades ago, I started going to Asian grocery stores, asking for advice and buying the different spices and mixes, including a plastic tub of green curry paste that I now always have on hand. A few years ago, Anna and I were cooking at a hotel in Bangkok, and I had the opportunity to hang out with the room service chef as an observer. I got excited when an order came in for green curry and thought it would be my chance to see the real deal made from scratch, but she pulled out the same white tub of curry paste that I use back home!

1 lb (450 g) ground pork

½ cup (125 mL) dry bread crumbs

½ cup (125 mL) unsweetened shredded coconut

1 large egg

1 tsp (5 mL) fish sauce or salt

1 Tbsp (15 mL) vegetable oil

2 Tbsp (30 mL) green curry paste (available at Asian grocery stores)

1 can (14 oz/400 mL) coconut milk (any fat percentage)

¼ lb (115 g) fresh green beans, cut in bite-sized pieces (about 1 cup/250 mL)

½ red bell pepper, seeded and diced

1 small carrot, peeled and diced

Cooked jasmine rice, for serving

¼ cup (60 mL) loosely packed fresh cilantro leaves

½ lime, cut in 4 wedges

GROUND AND DICED

1   Mix the pork, bread crumbs, coconut, egg and fish sauce in a large bowl.

2   Heat the oil in a large, heavy-bottomed pan over medium-high heat. Stir in the curry paste for 2 to 3 minutes to draw out the flavors. Stir in the coconut milk, bring up to a simmer and then add the green beans, bell pepper and carrot.

3   Using a small ice-cream scoop or a spoon, portion and shape the pork mixture into meatballs and carefully drop them into the simmering liquid. Simmer in the sauce, uncovered (or the sauce with split), for 25 minutes. To test for doneness, break open a meatball—there should not be any visible pink, it should be firm to the touch on the outside and the internal temperature should be 165°F (74°C).

4   Serve the meatballs with steamed jasmine rice and sprinkled with fresh cilantro and lime juice.

Notes:

+   You can buy a range of Thai curry pastes for home cooking. Yellow is mildest and gets its color from turmeric; red is in the middle, with red chilies; and green is the hottest, with plenty of green chilies, cilantro and coconut. If your family is not into spicy hot, try this recipe with yellow curry paste to start.

YIELD: 6 SERVINGS
AS A MAIN

PREP TIME:
15 MINUTES

COOK TIME:
10 MINUTES

Little Max Cheeseburgers

LIVING HIGH OFF THE HOG

SPECIAL SAUCE

⅓ cup (80 mL) ketchup

⅓ cup (80 mL) mayonnaise

3 Tbsp (45 mL) sweet relish

2 Tbsp (30 mL) yellow mustard

½ tsp (2 mL) celery salt

BURGERS

2 lb (900 g) ground pork

1 tsp (5 mL) table salt

1 tsp (5 mL) ground black pepper

1 Tbsp (15 mL) vegetable oil

12 small dinner rolls or slider buns

Shredded iceberg lettuce, minced onions, sliced pickles and sliced cheddar cheese, for serving

My father, Max (Magnus), loved a good cheeseburger and would have loved these small but fully dressed double-decker ones. These burgers would also be great for a birthday party or family event. The size makes one just right for kids, but the grown-ups may find themselves coming up with a clever excuse to reach for a second.

———————

1 For the sauce, whisk together the ketchup, mayonnaise, relish, mustard and celery salt in a bowl. Chill until ready to assemble the burgers, or for up to 1 week.

2 For the burgers, mix the pork with the salt and pepper (using your hands is best) and divide the mixture into 12 portions. Shape each portion into a ball, flatten into a patty with your hands and transfer to a plate or baking sheet.

3 Heat a large skillet over medium-high heat and add the oil. Drop the patties into the pan (you may have to do this in batches) and cook until no pink is visible when you break one open a little, about 4 minutes per side.

4 To assemble, slice each roll horizontally into thirds. Generously spread the special sauce on the cut sides of each roll and place a cooked patty on the bottom and middle roll portions. Top the patties with your choice of lettuce, onions, pickles and cheese. Stack the rolls back together, covering with the top of the roll (you may need a skewer or pick to hold the burger together). Serve immediately.

Notes:

+ The cook time on these small burger patties is so quick that it's almost not worth heating up the grill, so I prefer to use a pan in the kitchen.

 YIELD: 4 SERVINGS

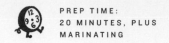 PREP TIME:
20 MINUTES, PLUS
MARINATING

 COOK TIME:
10 MINUTES

Boneless Loin Souvlaki on the Grill

with Tzatziki

When I was a culinary student in Toronto, I lived on the Danforth subway line in the Greek neighborhood. On occasion, I would treat myself to a real, sit-down meal in one of the area's restaurants. I loved the salty tang of olives and feta cheese, but the real treat was the grilled souvlaki, with its cool, lemony cucumber sauce. I think the chef knew I was a broke college kid, because I always seemed to get an extra helping of potatoes and rice.

1 Cut the pork loin into 1-inch (2.5 cm) pieces and put into a dish to marinate with the lemon juice, onion, oil, garlic, oregano and pepper Cover and refrigerate for at least 2 hours or up to 12 hours.

2 Soak the bamboo skewers in water for 1 hour; this will help prevent them from burning on the grill. Season the pork with the salt, then thread the meat onto the skewers. Leave a space at the blunt end as a handle, but make sure the sharp end of the skewer is covered by the pork to avoid scorching.

3 For the tzatziki, stir the yogurt with the cucumber, garlic, mint, lemon juice, oil and salt, and chill until ready to serve.

4 Heat the grill to medium-high and fold a 12-inch (30 cm) sheet of foil twice to make a 3-inch (8 cm) strip. Place this strip on the grill to protect the "handles" of the bamboo skewers and lay the skewers on the grill side by side so the handles are all on the foil. Cook until brown and firm to the touch, about 4 minutes per side.

5 Serve the hot souvlaki with the rice, pita bread, lemon wedges and tzatziki.

1 lb (450 g) boneless pork loin roast

Juice of 1 lemon

1 small red onion, grated

2 Tbsp (30 mL) olive oil

2 cloves garlic, minced

2 tsp (10 mL) dried oregano

1 tsp (5 mL) ground black pepper

8 six-inch (15 cm) bamboo skewers

1 tsp (5 mL) coarse salt

TZATZIKI

1 cup (250 mL) Greek yogurt (0% MF is fine)

½ English cucumber, seeds removed, grated and squeezed to remove water

1 clove garlic, minced

⅓ cup (80 mL) chopped fresh mint leaves

2 Tbsp (30 mL) fresh lemon juice

1 Tbsp (15 mL) olive oil

½ tsp (2 mL) coarse salt

4 cups (1 L) cooked yellow rice, for serving

Pita bread and lemon wedges, for serving

Notes:

+ Oregano is one of the few herbs I prefer to purchase dried. Rub it between your fingers to release the citrus-eucalyptus aromas to wake up marinades and dressings. If you're making the tzatziki ahead, add the salt to the grated cucumbers and let them sit for 30 minutes in the fridge, then squeeze out the extra water this will keep them crispy in the yogurt overnight. To make yellow rice, just add 1 tsp turmeric.

 YIELD: 8 SERVINGS
AS AN APPETIZER

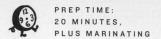 PREP TIME:
20 MINUTES,
PLUS MARINATING

 COOK TIME:
10 MINUTES

Spiedini

with Garlic & Rosemary

LIVING HIGH OFF THE HOG

SPIEDINI

16 six-inch (15 cm) bamboo
skewers

1 lb (450 g) boneless pork
loin, center cut

1 Tbsp (15 mL) olive oil

1 clove fresh garlic,
minced

2 tsp (10 mL) chopped
fresh rosemary

1 tsp (5 mL) ground black
pepper

1 tsp (5 mL) fine salt

FOR GRILLING

1 Tbsp (15 mL) olive oil

2 Tbsp (30 mL) chopped
fresh Italian parsley

1 Tbsp (15 mL) balsamic
vinegar

1 fresh rosemary sprig,
plus extra for serving

Lemon wedges, for serving

I've only had spiedini standing up! Unlike the hearty souvlaki that goes with salads or potatoes, these Italian-inspired grilled skewers are ideal as a starter for an outdoor party in the yard or at the cottage. And sometimes big flavors come in small packages.

1 Soak the bamboo skewers in water for 1 hour; this will help prevent them from burning on the grill.

2 Trim the pork of extra fat and silver skin (see page 21 for tips), and cut into small, bite-sized pieces. Toss the pork with the oil, garlic, rosemary, pepper and salt. Marinate in the fridge for at least 10 minutes and up to 2 hours.

3 Thread the pork onto the bamboo skewers. Leave a space at the blunt end for a handle but make sure the sharp end of the skewer is covered by the pork to avoid scorching.

4 For grilling, mix the olive oil, parsley and vinegar in a small dish. Heat the grill to medium-high and fold a 12-inch (30 cm) sheet of foil twice to make a 3-inch (8 cm) strip. Place this on the grill to protect the "handles" of the bamboo skewers and lay the skewers on the grill side by side so the handles are all on the foil. Use the rosemary sprig as a brush, dipping into the oil-parsley mixture and basting the spiedini as they grill. Grill the spiedini until they reach an internal temperature of 155°F (68°C), 4 minutes per side.

5 Serve on a platter with the lemon wedges and rosemary garnish.

Notes:

+ The perfume of rosemary comes through when the dressing is brushed onto the meat with a rosemary sprig. I like to drop bits of rosemary onto the grill to get little puffs of herb smoke over the meat.

Saigon Pork Rice Bowl

This one-bowl meal comes together in a hurry and is colorful and healthy enough that it satisfies both adventurous and picky eaters. It's also an approachable way to bring Vietnamese cooking styles home. The balance of sweet versus heat and the colors of the mango, herbs and vegetables are really fresh and appealing.

1   Heat the oil in a skillet over medium-high heat, then add the pork and onion. Sauté until the onion softens (the pork won't be cooked), 3 to 4 minutes. Stir in the garlic, ginger, brown sugar, fish sauce and hot sauce, and cook, reducing the heat to medium if the pork begins to stick, until the pork is no longer pink, any liquid evaporates, and the pork begins to caramelize, about 10 minutes more.

2   Remove the pan from the heat and stir in the carrot and bell pepper just to warm but not fully cook them. Stir in the lime juice and then taste to see if it needs any more salt or hot sauce.

3   To serve, divide the rice among 4 bowls, spoon the pork overtop and dress with the hoisin, sriracha, cucumber, mango and green onions. Finally, top with the cilantro and peanuts.

2 tsp (10 mL) vegetable oil

1 lb (450 g) ground pork

½ medium onion, sliced

1 clove garlic, minced

1 Tbsp (15 mL) finely grated fresh ginger

1 Tbsp (15 mL) packed light brown or cane sugar

Fish sauce or salt, to taste

Hot sauce, to taste

1 medium carrot, julienned

½ red bell pepper, seeded and julienned

Juice of 1 lime

3 cups (750 mL) cooked jasmine rice

Hoisin sauce

Sriracha sauce

¼ English cucumber, thinly sliced

½ mango, peeled and sliced

2 green onions, thinly sliced

Fresh cilantro leaves and chopped peanuts, for sprinkling

Mexican Chorizo Taco Mix

for Nachos, Salads and More

2 tsp (10 mL) vegetable
    oil

1 lb (450 g) ground pork

1 Tbsp (15 mL) ground
    cumin

1 tsp (5 mL) mild
    Hungarian paprika

1 tsp (5 mL) ground
    coriander

1 tsp (5 mL) chopped fresh
    thyme, leaves only

1 tsp (5 mL) crushed
    garlic

1 tsp (5 mL) coarse salt

1 tsp (5 mL) ground black
    pepper

½ tsp (2 mL) ground
    cinnamon

½ tsp (2 mL) dried
    oregano

¼ tsp (1 mL) ground cloves

¼ tsp (1 mL) cayenne
    pepper

2 Tbsp (30 mL) white wine
    vinegar

This style of chorizo is entirely different from the cured salami style that one associates with Spain. Rather, this recipe produces a scrambled meat mixture similar to taco filling, and it can be used for many dishes in Mexican cooking: right now, you should be dreaming of burritos, tacos, enchiladas and great nacho platters.

———————

1   Heat a large, heavy-bottomed skillet over medium heat and add the oil. Add the ground pork and cook, stirring often, until it begins to break down, about 5 minutes. Stir in the cumin, paprika, coriander, thyme, garlic, salt, pepper, cinnamon, oregano, cloves and cayenne, and cook until well-mixed and aromatic, 2 to 3 minutes. Stir in the vinegar and cook until the meat is no longer pink, 8 to 10 minutes more.

2   The chorizo can be prepared up to 2 days ahead and chilled, then reheated over medium heat before serving. This filling is at the heart of an easy, casual dinner around the kitchen island—just set up the usual taco kit of tortillas, lettuce, cheese, salsa, sour cream, hot sauce and whatever else your heart desires.

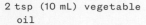

Notes:

+   Fresh thyme is always in my fridge because it has so many uses, but oregano is one herb that I prefer dried. Keep it tightly sealed for up to 6 months in the pantry.

Sausage Burgers

with Espresso Glazed Onions

131

GROUND AND D CED

A relaxed Sunday brunch at home with good friends and a couple of bottles of rosé is just what the doctor ordered, and this recipe is the prescription for contentment. The idea of combining coffee and onions came up innocently: while caramelizing onions, I needed a liquid to deglaze the pan, and a leftover shot of espresso in the stovetop moka was the closest thing within reach. The sweet onions balanced by the sharp, bitter taste and rich, toasty aroma of the coffee cried out for full prominence in a dish. The rest just fell into place.

1   Stir the sausage with the bread crumbs, Parmigiano-Reggiano and egg until well-combined (using your hands is easiest). Divide and shape the sausage mixture into 6 balls, rolling each one between your palms and flattening it into a patty as wide as the bun on which you plan to serve it. Stack the burgers between layers of parchment paper or plastic wrap, and chill until ready to cook (can be made up to 1 day ahead).

2   Heat 2 tsp (10 mL) of the olive oil in a heavy-bottomed skillet over medium-high heat. Add the onions and salt. Cook, stirring often, until the onions are soft and golden brown, about 35 minutes. Stir in the espresso, and cook until absorbed, 1 minute more. Set the pan aside to let the onions cool. You can also prepare this ahead and chill until ready to serve.

2 lb (900 g) mild Italian sausage, casings removed

½ cup (125 mL) dry bread crumbs

½ cup (125 mL) finely grated Parmigiano-Reggiano cheese

1 large egg

4 tsp (20 mL) olive oil, divided

4 cups (1 L) thinly sliced yellow onions

½ tsp (2 mL) table salt

¼ cup (60 mL) espresso coffee

6 egg buns

6 slices jack or cheddar cheese

½ cup (125 mL) grainy mustard

6 lettuce leaves, washed and dried

CONTINUES

Notes:

+   Buy freshly made sausage from your local independent butcher the first time you try this, but then get adventurous and make your own sausage blend at home with freshly ground meat (page 131). You can also cook the burgers on a grill for an outdoor brunch alfresco.

3   Heat the remaining 2 tsp (10 mL) of the olive oil in a heavy-bottomed skillet over medium heat and drop in the burger patties. Cook until no longer pink and the meat reaches an internal temperature of 165°F (74°C), about 5 minutes per side. Top each patty with a slice of jack cheese and a spoonful of the espresso onions while the burgers are still in the pan. Cover the pan and remove it from the heat to allow the onions and cheese to warm up.

4   To assemble, split the buns, toasting them if you wish. Assemble the burgers, topped with plenty of grainy mustard and crisp lettuce leaves.

Sausage Patties

Sausage is something that can be made at home, but special equipment is needed for grinding and stuffing. These patties do not have the familiar shape of the casing, but you can buy freshly ground pork and season with a variety of spices, then form into patties that can be used for breakfasts or incredible sandwiches, or served as a main with sides. You'll be pleased with the results, and the recipes are easy to put together and cook. I mean, what's the *wurst* that could happen?

For the following five variations on sausage patties, you'll follow the same directions for the method, as listed below.

1   In a mixing bowl or the bowl of a stand mixer fitted with the paddle attachment, stir the ground pork with all of the ingredients except the water until well-combined—if mixing manually in a bowl, using your hands works best. Drizzle in the cold water while mixing and make sure it is fully incorporated. Cover and chill until ready to cook.

2   Divide the meat mixture into 6 even portions and place each portion between 2 sheets of plastic wrap or in a cut-open reseal-able plastic bag. Flatten the patties with your hands to a thickness of ½ inch (1 cm) or to the diameter of the bun.

3   To cook, heat a heavy-bottomed skillet over medium-high heat and add the patties, leaving 1 inch (2.5 cm) between them. Reduce the heat to medium and cook until the patties are firm and the juices run clear, about 4 minutes per side.

CONTINUES

Sausage Variations

Canuck

1 lb (450 g) ground pork

3 Tbsp (45 mL) finely chopped dried cranberries

2 Tbsp (30 mL) maple syrup

½ tsp (2 mL) dried sage

1 tsp (5 mL) coarse salt

1 tsp (5 mL) ground black pepper

1 tsp (5 mL) rye whiskey

¼ cup (60 mL) cold water

-

Serve on a toasted English muffin with maple mustard and kettle chips.

Eye-Opener

1 lb (450 g) ground pork

3 Tbsp (45 mL) grated old cheddar cheese

2 Tbsp (30 mL) honey

1 clove garlic, minced

1 Tbsp (15 mL) dried chili flakes

1 Tbsp (15 mL) paprika

1 tsp (5 mL) coarse salt

1 tsp (5 mL) ground black pepper

¼ cup (60 mL) cold water

-

Serve on a dinner roll with steak sauce and pickled beets.

Korean

1 lb (450 g) ground pork

2 Tbsp (30 mL) gochujang chili paste (available at Asian grocery stores)

1 Tbsp (15 mL) toasted sesame seeds

1 clove garlic, minced

2 green onions, thinly sliced

1 tsp (5 mL) sesame oil

1 tsp (5 mL) ground black pepper

¼ cup (60 mL) cold water

-

Serve on a steamed bao bun with kimchi and sliced green onions.

Mediterranean

1 lb (450 g) ground pork

3 Tbsp (45 mL) finely chopped oil-packed sun-dried tomatoes

3 Tbsp (45 mL) crumbled feta cheese

2 Tbsp (30 mL) finely chopped pitted black olives

1 tsp (5 mL) finely grated lemon zest

1 Tbsp (15 mL) fresh lemon juice

1 tsp (5 mL) dried oregano

1 tsp (5 mL) ground black pepper

¼ cup (60 mL) cold water

-

Serve on a mini pita with cucumber slices, red onion rings and pitted black olives.

Spanish

1 lb (450 g) ground pork

2 Tbsp (30 mL) smoked paprika

2 Tbsp (30 mL) chopped fresh parsley

1 clove garlic, minced

1 tsp (5 mL) coarse salt

1 tsp (5 mL) ground black pepper

1 tsp (5 mL) finely grated orange zest

¼ cup (60 mL) cold water

-

Serve on a crusty roll with Manchego cheese and piquillo or roasted peppers.

Rigatoni

with Sausage & Sweet Peppers in Tomato Sauce

Apprentice cooks look up to their chef as a boss, teacher and mentor. When I was first starting out, I worked for a real character named Freddy, who was very tough on us during service but would always shake our hands and say thanks at the end of the shift. He had the ability to make very simple dishes taste absolutely delicious—this is one I remember him by.

1 Heat the oil in a large skillet or saucepot over medium-high heat. Add the sausage, onion and bell peppers, and cook, stirring and breaking up the sausage into bite-sized pieces, for 5 minutes. Add the garlic and dried chili flakes (if using) and cook until the onion and bell peppers are soft but not browned, 2 to 3 minutes more. Add the tomato sauce and reduce the heat to medium. Simmer, uncovered, until the sausage is fully cooked and the vegetables are tender, about 10 minutes.

2 Boil the pasta in a large pot of salted water over high heat according to the package directions. Reserve ½ cup (125 mL) of the pasta water and drain the pasta in a colander. Add the reserved pasta water to the tomato sauce. Toss the cooked pasta with the sauce, and stir in the cheese and basil. Season to taste and serve.

1 Tbsp (15 mL) olive oil

1 lb (450 g) fresh mild Italian sausage, casings removed

1 medium onion, cut in 1-inch (2.5 cm) dice

2 red and/or yellow bell peppers, seeded and cut in 1-inch (2.5 cm) dice

1 clove garlic, minced

½ tsp (2 mL) dried chili flakes (optional)

3 cups (750 mL) good-quality prepared tomato sauce

1 lb (450 g) dry rigatoni pasta

½ cup (125 mL) grated Parmigiano-Reggiano cheese

2 Tbsp (30 mL) fresh basil leaves, torn

Salt and pepper

137

GROUND AND DICED

Notes:

+ For a party, put this pasta into a big casserole dish and keep warm in the oven, and then set it out on the buffet table with extra cheese and dried chili flakes.

Chili

to Celebrate the New Big Screen

138

LIVING HIGH OFF THE HOG

2 Tbsp (30 mL) vegetable oil

1 medium onion, diced

1 large carrot, peeled and diced

1 stalk celery, diced

1 red bell pepper, seeded and diced

2 cloves garlic, minced

1 lb (450 g) ground pork

2 Tbsp (30 mL) chili powder

1 tsp (5 mL) ground cumin

1 tsp (5 mL) ground coriander

½ tsp (2 mL) ground cinnamon

½ cup (125 mL) beer or water

1 can (14 oz/398 mL) baked beans (I like chipotle-flavored)

1 can (28 oz/796 mL) diced tomatoes

½ cup (125 mL) raisins

½ cup (125 mL) shelled pumpkin seeds

Salt and pepper

Grated cheddar cheese, sour cream, lime wedges and hot sauce, for serving

A spectacular chili is warranted to match the excitement and energy of feeding a crowd for a big game or family gathering, or maybe when you get a new giant screen! This version uses plenty of vegetables and has a slight fruity character from the raisins and the pleasant crunch of pumpkin seeds. The ground pork is a sponge for the aromas of the spices and the sweet heat of the chipotle beans.

_____

1   Heat the oil in a large skillet over medium-high heat and sauté the onion, carrot, celery and bell pepper until softened, about 7 minutes. Stir in the garlic and reduce the heat to medium. Stir in the ground pork, chili powder, cumin, coriander and cinnamon. Cook, stirring to break up the pork and work in the spices, for 5 minutes. Stir in the beer, baked beans and tomatoes, then return to a gentle simmer, still over medium heat. Stir in the raisins and pumpkin seeds. Cover and reduce the heat further (if needed) to a low simmer. Cook, stirring occasionally, until the vegetables are tender and the sauce clings to them, about 20 minutes. Season to taste.

2   Serve the chili topped with your choice of cheese, sour cream, lime juice and hot sauce.

Notes:

+ Leftovers can be made into great hot sandwich buns or used as a topping for nachos. This is also a good make-ahead recipe: it can be cooked before your guests arrive and simply kept on low heat in a pot or slow cooker.

YIELD: 4 SERVINGS
AS A MAIN, 8 AS AN
APPETIZER

PREP TIME:
10 MINUTES

COOK TIME:
20 MINUTES

Caramelized Chili Pork

with Peanuts & Lime

This quick-cook diced pork can be used to top a rice or noodle bowl. It has an amazing balance of bitter and sweet from the beer caramel, along with punchy heat and ginger notes. This is a dish that will have your friends and family wondering when you became such a great Thai cook.

---

1 Heat the oil in a heavy-bottomed skillet over high heat. Add the pork, making sure to brown on all sides. Once browned, remove the pork to a plate (it won't be cooked through). Reduce the heat to medium and add the shallots, garlic, ginger, hot chili, bell pepper and celery. Cook, stirring, until the shallots are softened and lightly browned to a golden color, about 5 minutes. Stir in the beer and brown sugar, then turn up the heat to medium-high and boil, stirring occasionally, until reduced to a syrup consistency and the bubbles are quite small, 5 to 10 minutes. Add the pork back to the sauce, stir well, and season with the fish sauce and sriracha. Cook until the pork is cooked through and the sauce coats it like a glaze, 2 to 3 minutes more.

2 Serve with the rice and sugar snap peas, topped with the green onion, peanuts, cilantro leaves and lime.

1 Tbsp (15 mL) vegetable oil

1 lb (450 g) diced pork sirloin or center-cut loin (silver skin removed; see page 21)

3 shallots, sliced

2 cloves garlic, minced

1 Tbsp (15 mL) finely grated fresh ginger

1 hot Thai chili, split

½ red bell pepper, seeded and diced

1 stalk celery, diced

¾ cup (175 mL) lager beer or water

⅓ cup (80 mL) packed dark brown sugar

Fish sauce or salt

Sriracha sauce

4 cups (1 L) cooked jasmine rice

3 cups (750 mL) cooked sugar snap peas

Sliced green onion, chopped peanuts, fresh cilantro leaves and lime wedges, for serving

141

GROUND AND DICED

Notes:

+ To serve this as an appetizer, use whole lettuce leaves as wraps. Fill with the spicy meat mix and top with the sauce, herbs and peanuts for a handheld package of explosive flavors. You can also use up leftover cooked pork roast by cooking it in this sauce. Dice and add from the point of searing the meat.

Hot Italian Sausage

with Garlic Rapini & Peppers on Polenta

2 cups (500 mL) 2% milk

1 cup (250 mL) cornmeal

¼ cup (60 mL) finely grated Parmigiano-Reggiano cheese

1 Tbsp (15 mL) butter

1½ lb (675 g) fresh hot Italian sausage (4 large)

1 red bell pepper, seeded and cut in strips

Salt

1 bundle fresh rapini, trimmed

2 Tbsp (30 mL) olive oil

1 clove garlic, minced

½ lemon

The combination of spicy sausage, bitter green vegetables and cheesy polenta is a version of comfort food that I found as an adult. I didn't grow up eating Italian food but learned to love the bold flavors and simple, classic combinations. This dish is ideal for a weeknight dinner with friends but also leaves great leftovers—if there are any.

---

1   Heat the milk and 2 cups (500 mL) of water in a saucepot over high heat. Sprinkle in the cornmeal while stirring continuously. When the cornmeal starts to bubble, reduce the heat to a gentle simmer and cook, stirring often, until it is a thick porridge that mounds up when scooped with a spoon, about 25 minutes. Stir in the cheese and butter, then cover to keep warm until ready to eat.

2   Meanwhile, cook the sausages in a dry skillet over medium heat until some of the fat starts to come out, turning them so they brown on all sides, about 5 minutes. Add the bell pepper and a pinch of salt and cook until the sausage is firm, the juices run clear and the sausage reaches an internal temperature of 165°F (74°C), about 5 minutes more.

3   Bring 12 cups (3 L) of salted water to a boil, blanch the rapini for 2 minutes to make it dark green and tender, then drain in a colander. If you are not using the rapini right away, it can be transferred to an ice-water bath to stop cooking.

4   Cook the garlic in the olive oil in a large frying pan over medium heat to release the aromas, 2 to 3 minutes. Add the rapini, stir to coat and season with lemon juice and salt.

5   To serve, ladle a scoop of polenta onto a plate then add one-quarter of the rapini and 1 sausage with peppers per person.

Notes:

+   I like extra-hot flavors, so I serve this with an Italian chili condiment like La Bomba or with pickled hot pepper rings. Crusty bread, a tossed salad and a bottle of red wine rounds this meal out nicely. Lastly, try adding Gorgonzola cheese instead of Parmigiano-Reggiano for a different taste for the polenta.

YIELD: 12 SERVINGS
MAKES TWO
9 X 5-INCH (2 L)
MEATLOAVES

PREP TIME:
10 MINUTES

COOK TIME:
1 HOUR 10 MINUTES

Joe Meatloaf

This is an unassuming name for a dish, but the flavor is anything but. The tangy dill pickle accent, sweet glaze and rich, meaty texture make this a really good meatloaf but an even better sandwich the next day. I also have a fancy bacon weave meatloaf (Bacon Wrapped Meatloaf with Orange Marmalade & Beer Glaze, page 146), but this one is, you know, just Joe Meatloaf.

1 Preheat the oven to 325°F (160°C). Line two 9 x 5-inch (2 L) loaf tins with parchment paper, with a little overhang to make removal easier.

2 Soak the bread crumbs in the milk until the milk has been absorbed, about 10 minutes. Stir in the eggs, relish, salt and Worcestershire sauce. Add the ground pork and mix thoroughly (using your hands is easiest), making sure everything is well-combined. Pack the meatloaf into the prepared tins and press down with the back side of a fork to force out any air pockets. Bake the meatloaves until the internal temperature reaches 160°F (71°C), 45 to 55 minutes.

3 While the meatloaves are cooking, prepare the glaze by whisking together the ketchup, brown sugar and Worcestershire sauce. After 45 minutes, baste the tops of the meatloaves with the glaze and bake until the meatloaves reach an internal temperature of 165°F (74°C), about 15 minutes more. Remove the meatloaves to a cooling rack and let them rest for 5 minutes before slicing. If you like, the second meatloaf can be tightly wrapped in plastic once it has cooled, and frozen for up to 4 months.

2 cups (500 mL) dry bread crumbs

1 cup (250 mL) 2% milk

2 large eggs

1 cup (250 mL) dill pickle relish or diced dill pickles

2 tsp (10 mL) coarse salt

4 dashes Worcestershire sauce

2¼ lb (1 kg) ground pork

GLAZE

½ cup (125 mL) ketchup

¼ cup (60 mL) packed light brown sugar

4 dashes (15 mL) Worcestershire sauce

145

GROUND AND DICED

Notes:

+ I've found that actual oven temperatures can vary from what you set it to. To verify you have your oven set correctly, place an oven thermometer (an inexpensive item) at the back corner of the oven and keep tabs on it as you cook and bake.

Bacon Wrapped Meatloaf

with Orange Marmalade & Beer Glaze

2½ lb (1.1 kg) ground pork

1 cup (250 mL) dry bread crumbs

1½ cups (375 mL) wheat beer, divided

2 large eggs

3 Tbsp (45 mL) sweet pickle relish

2 Tbsp (30 mL) grainy mustard

4 dashes (15 mL) Worcestershire sauce

1 tsp (5 mL) coarse salt

6 strips bacon

½ cup (125 mL) orange marmalade

Craft beer fans will rush the stage to get near this hopster-inspired flying cigar of deliciousness. The free-form loaf is wrapped in bacon and glazed with orange marmalade and beer to finish off with a hoppy, sweet aromatic tang. Now, where did I put my plaid Jack shirt, ironic toque and clip-on beard?

————————

1 Preheat the oven to 350°F (180°C).

2 Stir together the pork, bread crumbs, 1 cup (250 mL) of the beer, eggs, relish, mustard, Worcestershire and salt in a bowl until well-combined (using your hands is easiest). Cover and refrigerate while preparing the bacon.

3 Line a baking sheet with parchment paper and make a "grid" of the bacon strips by making an "X" with 2 strips of bacon from corner to corner on the parchment, then adding the others, leaving a space between each as wide as a strip of bacon (1). You'll end up with what looks like an overlapping "XXX," with 3 strips running one way corner to corner and the other 3 perpendicular to them. Remove the meatloaf mix from the fridge and shape into a cylinder the length of the bacon lattice (2). Lift one end of the parchment to roll the bacon over the meatloaf mix to meet at the other side (3). Slide the meatloaf to the middle of the pan so the seam of the bacon lattice is underneath the meatloaf, on top of the parchment paper.

4 Bake in the oven for 1 hour, and then stir the marmalade and remaining ½ cup (125 mL) beer together. Spoon the mixture over the meatloaf and bake until the glaze is sticky and the meat has reached an internal temperature of 165°F (74°C), about 15 minutes more.

5 Remove from the oven and rest for 5 minutes before slicing.

Notes:

+ You can pull together a great blind tasting of craft beers by buying a dozen varieties in tall cans, showing different styles and points of origin—and don't forget to put in a couple of ringers. Cover the cans in paper so your guests can't see the labels, and then taste and discuss, revealing the labels afterward.

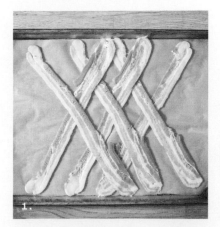

1.

2.

3.

Mapo Tofu

Spicy Braised Pork with Tofu

This "Grandma's Tofu" is inspired by my old buddy Toshi, who worked and lived with Anna and me for a couple of years before returning to Tokyo. He would make this one-pot meal on days off and then reheat it for late-night after-work snacks. It is mild and comforting but also has a little sweet and spicy "wow" factor going on.

———

1   Heat the oil in a large skillet and sauté the pork, onion and celery over medium-high heat, stirring occasionally, until the onion is translucent, about 5 minutes. Add the garlic, ginger and chili flakes, and cook until the garlic is browned, 3 to 5 minutes. Stir in the stock, brown sugar, black bean sauce and soy sauce. Bring to a full boil, then reduce the heat to a gentle simmer and cook until the pork is fully cooked, about 5 minutes. Gently stir in the diced tofu to heat it through, but don't break it down too much. Cook for 5 more minutes to make sure the tofu is piping hot.

2   Blend the cornstarch into 2 Tbsp (30 mL) of cold water, add to the tofu mixture and stir gently—the liquid will thicken once the sauce begins to bubble, then develops a shine and sticks to the tofu.

3   Top with the green onions and serve over cooked rice and steamed greens, such as bok choy.

2 tsp (10 mL) vegetable oil

1 lb (450 g) ground pork

1 medium onion, diced

1 stalk celery, diced

1 clove garlic, minced

1 Tbsp (15 mL) minced ginger

2 tsp (10 mL) dried chili flakes

1½ cups (375 mL) chicken stock or water

¼ cup (60 mL) packed light brown sugar

2 Tbsp (30 mL) garlic black bean sauce (I like Lee Kum Kee)

1 Tbsp (15 ml) soy sauce

1 pkg (400 g) firm tofu, cut in ½-inch (1 cm) dice

2 Tbsp (30 mL) cornstarch

2 green onions, thinly sliced

4 cups cooked short-grain rice, for serving

Steamed bok choy, for serving (optional)

GROUND AND DICED

149

Notes:

+   This dish is popular in Japan but originally comes from China, and I've had versions in Hong Kong that are absolutely electric with Szechuan pepper and chilies—it was an Asian version of the best chili con carne you could imagine.

Fricassee

with White Turnips, Carrots, Riesling & Leeks

2 Tbsp (30 mL) oil

3 Tbsp (45 mL) all-purpose flour

2 cups (500 mL) chicken stock

1 cup (250 mL) Riesling wine

1½ lb (675 g) lean pork shoulder, cut in 1-inch (2.5 cm) pieces

3-4 white turnips, peeled and cut in large dice

1 leek, white and light green parts only, washed and cut in 2-inch (5 cm) slices

2 carrots, peeled and cut in large dice

2 sprigs fresh thyme

½ cup (125 mL) 35% whipping cream

Salt and pepper

2 Tbsp (30 mL) chopped parsley, for sprinkling

4 crusty rolls, for serving

A fricassee is a white stew—the sauce in this braised dish is finished off with a luxurious hit of rich cream to round out the flavor, give the cooking juices a silky finish and maintain a creamy white color (unlike so many sauces, which are brown). The aromatic hints of spice come from the fragrant leeks and turnips. It will only get better when you reheat it for lunch the next day.

———

1   Preheat the oven to 325°F (160°C).

2   Heat the oil in a heavy-bottomed skillet or Dutch oven over medium heat. Stir in the flour with a wooden spoon to make a roux. Cook, stirring, until the roux takes on a "sandy" look but does not color, about 5 minutes.

3   Reduce the heat to low and slowly whisk in the stock, followed by the wine, to avoid any lumps. Return to medium heat and stir in the diced pork, turnips, leek, carrots and thyme. Bring to a simmer while stirring, cover and transfer to the oven. Cook until the meat breaks apart when you press it against the side of the pot with a spoon, about 1 hour. You can simmer the fricassee over low heat on the stovetop, covered, stirring occasionally, if you prefer, as it cooks for the same amount of time.

4   Remove the pan from the oven and stir to check the consistency—the sauce should coat the back of a spoon and cling to the meat and vegetables. Return to the stove and add the cream in a steady stream while stirring. Bring just to a gentle simmer and season to taste. Sprinkle with the parsley and serve with the crusty rolls.

Notes:

+   Shoulder is the ideal cut for the diced meat in this stew because the extra fat keeps it moist over the long, slow braise time.

Pork Carbonnade

with Prunes & Dark Beer

This stew is influenced by the cuisine of Belgium (where it is typically made with beef) and needs a punch of full-bodied dark beer to lend color and richness to the sauce. The prunes are not distinguishable in the finished sauce but make a beautiful bridge between stew and brew. This recipe is ideal for an autumn weekend lunch or dinner after a day outdoors.

1 Preheat the oven to 325°F (160°C).

2 Add 1 Tbsp (15 mL) of the oil to a large heavy-bottomed pot over medium-high heat. Toss the diced pork with the flour and season with salt and pepper. Shake off any excess flour and brown the pork in the hot pan in a single layer, stirring occasionally, until it has browned on all sides, 2 to 3 minutes. (You may have to do this in 2 batches, adding the remaining oil when needed.) Once browned, remove the pork to a bowl.

3 Reduce the heat to medium and add the onion, celery, carrot and mushrooms. Cook, stirring, until the onion is translucent, about 5 minutes. Return the browned pork as well as any remaining flour to the pan and cook, stirring, for 1 minute more. Add the beef stock, beer and prunes. Stir and bring to a full simmer, then reduce the heat to medium-low so that it simmers gently. Cover and place in the oven for until the meat is tender but not falling apart, about 1½ hours. Remove the pan from the oven, stir in the vinegar and brown sugar, and season to taste.

4 Sprinkle with parsley and serve with crusty bread and more of the same beer.

2 Tbsp (30 mL) vegetable oil, divided

1½ lb (675 g) pork shoulder, cut in 1-inch (2.5 cm) cubes

¼ cup (60 mL) all-purpose flour

Salt and pepper

½ medium onion, diced

½ stalk celery, diced

1 small carrot, peeled and diced

½ lb (250 g) cremini mushrooms, quartered

2 cups (500 mL) low-sodium beef stock

1 cup (250 mL) dark beer

½ cup (125 mL) quartered pitted prunes

1 Tbsp (15 mL) red wine vinegar

1 Tbsp (15 mL) packed light brown sugar

2 Tbsp (30 mL) chopped parsley, for sprinkling

Crusty bread, for serving

Notes:

+ The addition of the sugar and vinegar at the end wakes up the sauce and gives a nice balance to the dish.

Tuesday Tacos

with Bell Peppers & Fresh Pineapple Salsa

LIVING HIGH OFF THE HOG

SALSA

1 cup (250 mL) diced fresh
  pineapple

½ cup (125 mL) diced fresh
  tomato

2 Tbsp (30 mL) chopped
  fresh cilantro

Salt and pepper

MEAT FILLING

1 lb (450 g) boneless pork
  loin

1 red bell pepper, seeded
  and diced

2 tsp (10 mL) kosher salt,
  plus more to taste

2 tsp (10 mL) ground cumin

1 tsp (5 mL) dried chili
  flakes

1 tsp (5 mL) dried oregano

1 Tbsp (15 mL) vegetable
  oil

2 tsp (10 mL) cornstarch

2 Tbsp (30 mL) fresh lemon
  juice

Ground black pepper

Small soft flour or corn
  tortillas, shredded
  cabbage, sour cream and
  hot sauce, for serving

Instead of hours of preparation and cooking, this is a quick recipe for dinner that can be served with a side salad, rice or just plenty of tortillas for a make-your-own taco meal.

1 For the salsa, stir together the pineapple, tomato and cilantro in a bowl and season to taste. Chill until ready to serve.

2 Trim extra fat and silver skin from the pork loin (see page 21 for tips), and cut it into bite-sized strips. Toss the pork in a bowl with the bell pepper, salt, cumin, chili flakes and oregano.

3 Heat the vegetable oil in a large skillet over medium-high heat and add in the meat mixture. Cook, stirring, until the bell pepper softens and the meat browns and is fully cooked (cut into a piece to check that the juices run clear), 8 to 10 minutes. Stir the cornstarch with 1 Tbsp (15 mL) of cold water and add it to the pan to thicken the sauce. Add the lemon juice and remove the pan from the heat to serve immediately.

4 To serve, spoon some of the meat filling into a warm tortilla and top with the pineapple salsa, cabbage, sour cream and hot sauce.

Notes:

+ Stack the tortillas and wrap them in foil in a low oven (250°F/120°C) to warm. Our pal Sam's mom in California kept tortillas warm in a beautiful embroidered napkin on the table—we do the same with a tea towel. Don't store any leftovers with the raw pineapple, as the enzymes will make the meat soft and pasty.

"View of the Danube" Paprikash

Traveling to a food festival in Budapest gave me an opportunity to experience the flavors of this classic culinary-rich city. I remember having the most romantic glass of champagne with Anna up on the citadel, looking down onto the Danube River and the lights of the city. And, of course, I remember the paprikash. Anna loves the depth of the onion and red pepper aroma in this recipe and absolutely has to have a dollop of sour cream on top. This hearty, Hungarian-inspired stew comes together in less than an hour and delivers a full, satisfying flavor that only gets better when you reheat it the next day.

2 tsp (10 mL) vegetable oil

1½ lb (675 g) diced lean pork shoulder, cut in 1-inch (2.5 cm) cubes

2 medium onions, diced

1 red bell pepper, seeded and diced

¼ cup (60 mL) sweet paprika

2 Tbsp (30 mL) all-purpose flour

2 cloves garlic, minced

1½ cups (375 mL) chicken stock

⅓ cup (80 mL) full-fat sour cream, plus extra for serving

Salt and pepper

About 6 cups (1.5 L) cooked egg noodles, for serving

Chopped fresh Italian parsley, for garnish

1 Heat the oil in a large pot over medium-high heat and sauté the pork and onions until the onions are soft and translucent, about 5 minutes. Stir in the bell pepper, paprika, flour and garlic, and continue to cook, stirring often, to toast the paprika and bring out the aroma, 3 to 5 minutes. Add the stock, bring to a full simmer and then reduce the heat to medium-low. Cover and simmer gently until the meat is fork-tender, about 40 minutes.

2 When ready to serve, remove the pan from the heat, stir in the sour cream and season to taste.

3 Serve over egg noodles, sprinkled with parsley, and add extra sour cream if you like.

Notes:

+ Paprika is powdered dried bell peppers that will thicken a broth when cooked into a stew. You can purchase sweet or hot, or even Spanish, which has a pronounced smoky character to it. Don't cover to simmer once you've added the sour cream. It will separate if you do.

Pork Sirloin Vindaloo

LIVING HIGH OFF THE HOG

2¼ lb (1 kg) boneless pork sirloin (chops or roast), cut in 1-inch (2.5 cm) cubes

3 Tbsp (45 mL) white wine vinegar

1 Tbsp (15 mL) ground cumin

1 Tbsp (15 mL) ground coriander

2 tsp (10 mL) dried chili flakes

2 tsp (10 mL) ground turmeric

2 tsp (10 mL) table salt, divided

1 tsp (5 mL) ground cinnamon

½ tsp (2 mL) ground cloves

½ tsp (2 mL) ground cardamom

2 Tbsp (30 mL) vegetable oil

4 medium onions, diced

2 Tbsp (30 mL) finely grated fresh ginger

2 cloves garlic, minced

1 can (28 oz/796 mL) diced tomatoes

Salt and pepper

Chopped fresh cilantro, for sprinkling

4 cups (1 L) cooked basmati rice

The aromas and kick of Indian food are so complex and deep in flavor—it is one of the great cuisines of the world. This style of recipe comes from Goa, a former Portuguese colony where chilies were introduced to the continent. Goa was also the only place in India that cooked pork in the old days. The name comes from the Portuguese recipe for meat "vinha d'alhos," a wine and garlic marinade, but the lack of wine in India gave way to using local vinegar and additional spices. In the old days, the fiery spices, garlic, vinegar and salt would have helped preserve the meat, but you won't have to worry about it lasting long in your kitchen.

1   Toss the pork with the vinegar, cumin, coriander, chili flakes, turmeric, 1 tsp (5 mL) salt, cinnamon, cloves and cardamom. Chill for at least 1 hour and up to 12 hours, covered, in the fridge. The longer you marinate the pork, the more intense the flavors will be.

2   Heat the oil in a large heavy-bottomed skillet over medium-high heat. Reduce the heat to medium and cook the onions with the remaining 1 tsp (5 mL) salt, stirring often, until they are soft, golden brown and smelling great, 10 to 15 minutes. Stir in the ginger and garlic, then add the marinated pork. Stir thoroughly and cook until the meat is evenly coated with the onions (don't worry if the meat doesn't brown), about 5 minutes. Stir in the tomatoes and 1 cup (250 mL) of water, bring to a simmer and cover. Lower the heat to a gentle simmer and cook, stirring occasionally, until the meat is tender, 30 to 40 minutes. Taste and season with more salt if needed.

3   Sprinkle with chopped cilantro and serve with basmati rice.

Notes:

+ You can buy or make your own naan to have on the side. Serve with the best-quality basmati rice, vegetables, chutney and pickles. You can also make Tzatziki (page 123) and add a pinch of ground cumin to create raita, a cooling yogurt sauce.

CHOPS AND STEAKS

MODEL: H **MANUFACTURER**: Berkel **YEAR**: 1940

NOTES: I started Olson Hardware after refurbishing an old beauty for our friend, Robert. The process includes totally rebuilding a machine and applying a powder coat finish. I named the project after my father, Max, who owned Olson's Hardware for 32 years.

Panko Crusted Tonkatsu

(Japanese Breaded Pork Cutlets)

I love the crunchy texture of the outside of these juicy cutlets. The crisp, cool vegetables pair nicely with the rich, sweet flavor of this "steak" sauce. Toasting the bread crumbs gives you great results without the mess of deep-frying, and you can use a mandoline to get professional-looking results on the vegetable cuts.

———————

1 For the accompaniments, mix the cucumber with the rice vinegar, sesame oil and salt, and chill until ready to eat. Chill the thinly sliced cabbage in ice-water to crisp for 20 minutes, then drain and pat dry with kitchen towels just before serving. Cut the lemon into 6 wedges and chill.

2 For the sauce, whisk together the ketchup, soy sauce and Worcestershire sauce, and pour into 6 little serving dishes.

3 Toast the panko in a dry skillet over medium heat, stirring often, until lightly browned, about 4 minutes. Then stir in the butter until melted.

4 Preheat the oven to 400°F (200°C). Line a baking sheet with foil or parchment paper and place a wire rack overtop.

5 Place each pork cutlet, one at a time, in a cut-open resealable plastic bag and pound with a meat mallet (or the bottom of a pot) until it is ½ inch (1 cm) thick. Season with salt and pepper, and chill until ready to cook.

6 Set up 3 bowls—the first for the flour, the second for the egg wash, and the third for the toasted panko bread crumbs. Dip each of the pork cutlets into the flour, shake off the excess, then dip into the egg and, finally, into the panko. Set the breaded cutlets on the wire rack set over the baking sheet and bake until golden brown and crispy, about 20 minutes. Check that the pork is cooked through by cutting into a cutlet. If the juices run clear, it's done.

ACCOMPANIMENTS

1 English cucumber, thinly sliced on a mandoline

2 Tbsp (30 mL) rice wine vinegar

1 tsp (5 mL) sesame oil

½ tsp (2 mL) table salt

4 cups (1 L) finely sliced green cabbage (sliced on a mandoline)

1 lemon

TONKATSU SAUCE

⅓ cup (80 mL) ketchup

2 Tbsp (30 mL) soy sauce

8–10 dashes Worcester-shire sauce

TONKATSU

3 cups (750 mL) panko bread crumbs

2 Tbsp (30 mL) butter

1½ lb (675 g) boneless pork loin, rib end, cut in 6 pieces

Salt and pepper

⅔ cup (160 mL) all-purpose flour

1 lightly whisked large egg + 2 Tbsp (30 mL) water

6 cups (1.5 L) cooked Japanese rice

3 Tbsp (45 mL) sesame seeds, toasted

7   To serve, slice each cutlet into 5 strips and serve with cooked
    Japanese rice, the Tonkatsu sauce, cucumber salad and a mound
    of the drained cabbage. Sprinkle the toasted sesame seeds over
    the cutlets, cucumber salad and cabbage.

After coating with breadcrumbs, the meat is baked, not fried.

Notes:

+   The rib end of the pork
    loin has dark meat with
    more marbling, which ends
    up staying juicy when
    cooked. Follow the package
    instructions when making
    Japanese short-grain rice:
    it will be sticky but not
    gluey, and its dense
    texture is the perfect foil
    for the crunchy cutlets.

 YIELD: 4 SERVINGS

 PREP TIME:
15 MINUTES,
PLUS MARINATING

 COOK TIME:
15 MINUTES

Chicken Fried Pork Steaks with Sausage Gravy

"Chicken frying" refers to dredging and frying meat in the same way you would for Southern fried chicken. These pork steaks are golden brown and tender, and just so satisfying with the sausage gravy on top. It's dinnertime, so pass the biscuits, cousin.

---

1   For the gravy, sauté the sausage meat in the butter in a saucepot over medium-high heat to cook through and release the oil, about 3 minutes. Reduce the heat to medium and add the flour. Cook, stirring, until the paste takes on a pleasant almond aroma but does not turn brown, about 3 minutes. Add about ½ cup (125 mL) of the milk while whisking and let it thicken before slowly adding the remaining milk, whisking constantly. Bring the gravy to a simmer over medium heat, whisking often, and cook until it has thickened, 4 to 5 minutes. Season to taste and keep warm over low heat. Alternatively, the gravy can be prepared ahead of time, chilled and reheated over medium heat.

2   Place each pork cutlet, one at a time, in a cut open resealable plastic bag and pound it with a meat mallet (or the bottom of a pot) until it is ½-inch (1 cm) thick. Whisk the buttermilk, garlic and salt in a flat dish and add the cutlets to marinate for 20 minutes in the fridge.

3   Heat the vegetable oil in a deep fryer to 350°F (180°C). Line a baking sheet with foil or parchment paper and place a wire rack on top. Preheat your oven to 300°F (150°C) to keep the cooked cutlets warm.

GRAVY

4 oz (120 g) fresh
   sausage, casings
   removed (I use hot
   Italian)

2 Tbsp (30 mL) butter

¼ cup (60 mL) all-purpose
   flour

2 cups (500 mL) 2% milk,
   divided

Salt and pepper

CHICKEN FRIED CUTLETS

8 pork cutlets from the
   leg, 3 oz (90 g) each

1 cup (250 mL) buttermilk

1 clove garlic, minced

1 tsp (5 mL) table salt

Vegetable oil, for frying

1 cup (250 mL) all-purpose
   flour

2 tsp (10 mL) ground black
   pepper

Biscuits, for serving
   (optional)

CHOPS AND STEAKS

CONTINUES

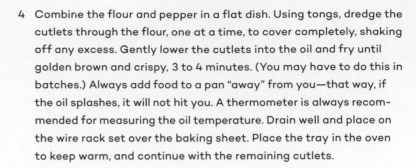

4   Combine the flour and pepper in a flat dish. Using tongs, dredge the cutlets through the flour, one at a time, to cover completely, shaking off any excess. Gently lower the cutlets into the oil and fry until golden brown and crispy, 3 to 4 minutes. (You may have to do this in batches.) Always add food to a pan "away" from you—that way, if the oil splashes, it will not hit you. A thermometer is always recommended for measuring the oil temperature. Drain well and place on the wire rack set over the baking sheet. Place the tray in the oven to keep warm, and continue with the remaining cutlets.

5   Serve the warm cutlets with the gravy on top. Freshly baked biscuits would be a wonderful side.

Notes:

+ We have a small countertop deep fryer, and I use it outside on the deck (to keep the oil odors from lingering inside). If you don't have a fryer, carefully do this on the stovetop using a deep pan, like a Dutch oven, and vegetable oil. Use a thermometer to carefully monitor your oil temperature, and be sure to let the oil come back up to temperature between batches.

Loin "Sangwich"

with Provolone, Red Onion & Hot Peppers on Ciabatta

2 Tbsp (30 mL) olive oil, divided

1 medium red onion, sliced

½ cup (125 mL) pickled banana pepper rings

1 lb (450 g) boneless pork loin, rib end

1 Tbsp (15 mL) Montreal steak spice

4 kaiser buns, split and lightly toasted

1 cup (250 mL) good-quality tomato sauce

8 slices provolone cheese

When I was in cooking school in Toronto, I'd work late at Le Sélect Bistro and then head out for fun with my pal Chris Zielinski. One of the last stops of the night would inevitably be for an Italian sandwich. The soft bun, juicy meat, cheese, tomato, onions and scorching hot peppers were so incredibly good. Standing on a sidewalk under the restaurant's neon sign and eating out of a paper napkin added the perfect touch of class.

_____

1   Preheat the oven to 350°F (180°C) and line a baking sheet with parchment paper.

2   Heat a sauté pan over medium heat and add 1 Tbsp (15 mL) of the olive oil. Add the onion and sauté until soft and tender, 8 to 10 minutes. Transfer the cooked onion to a bowl and toss with the pickled pepper rings. Set aside.

3   Cut the pork loin into 8 even slices. Place each pork cutlet, one at a time, in a cut-open resealable plastic bag and pound it with a meat mallet (or the bottom of a pot) until it is ½ inch (1 cm) thick. Season the pork cutlets with the Montreal steak spice on both sides and pan-fry in the remaining 1 Tbsp (15 mL) oil over high heat until cooked through, 2 to 3 minutes per side.

4   To assemble the "sangwiches," put the split buns on a tray, then spoon the onion-pepper mixture over the bottom. Place 2 cutlets overtop and top with the tomato sauce and cheese. Bake open-faced in the preheated oven to melt the cheese until it is bubbling, 5 to 8 minutes.

Notes:

+   You can add in your favorite toppings, like mushrooms, bacon, artichoke hearts, pickled eggplant or sun-dried tomatoes.

Pan Fried Loin Steaks

with Bell Peppers, Asparagus, Sweet Onions & Cherry Tomatoes

This main course is a one-pot meal of golden brown steaks bathed in a garlic tomato sauce and filled to the brim with fresh asparagus and sweet peppers. Gather the ingredients together, slice and dice, turn up the heat (and the music), and before you know it, dinner is ready. The steaks have a firm, meaty texture that will soak up the sauce.

1½ lb (675 g) boneless
pork loin steaks
(about 4)

Salt and pepper

1 Tbsp (15 mL) olive oil

2 red bell peppers,
seeded and diced

1 large Vidalia onion,
cut in large dice

1 lb (450 g) fresh asparagus, trimmed and cut in
1-inch (2.5 cm) pieces

1 cup (250 mL) cherry
tomatoes, halved

1 clove garlic, minced

1 tsp (5 mL) chopped fresh
thyme, leaves only

1 Tbsp (15 mL) balsamic
vinegar

Chopped fresh Italian
parsley, for sprinkling

1 Heat the oil in a large heavy-bottomed skillet over high heat. Season each side of the pork with salt and pepper, and brown for 4 minutes per side, then remove to a plate.

2 Add the bell peppers and onion to the pan, reduce the heat to medium, and cook, stirring often, until the onion softens, 5 to 8 minutes. Stir in the asparagus. Add the pork back to the pan, nestling it into the vegetables, and cook until done but still juicy in the center, 4 to 5 minutes. Add the cherry tomatoes, garlic, thyme and balsamic vinegar, and gently stir in around the pork. Cook until tomatoes are warmed through and pork reaches an internal temperature of 145°F (63°C), about 3 minutes. Season to taste.

3 To serve, place the pork on top of the vegetables and sprinkle with the parsley. Serve with a side of pasta, rice or salad and maybe a small cheese plate.

Notes:

+ Do all of your preparation before starting to cook, keep your prep area tidy and clean as you go. I like to cut all the vegetables first and put them into bowls near the stove along with all the other ingredients so that when I start cooking the meat, everything else is right in front of me. As the dishes empty, they go into the sink. Every time I have a couple of free minutes, I wash the dishes so the kitchen is basically already clean when dinner is ready to eat.

Pan Fried Tenderloin Medallions

with Apple Cider-Thyme Cream on Potato Cakes

When I drive past the pumpkin farm and think of stomping through the woods, kicking up leaves, this dish is what I crave once I get home. Pork tenderloin and apples are perfect partners when the autumn weather turns cool, meals are all indoors and we have a fresh crop of apples that are super sweet and juicy. I make sure every forkful has a piece of the crispy potato cake with pork and apple blanketed in the luxurious cream sauce.

1   Trim the silver skin from the tenderloins (see page 21 for tips) and cut each into 6 portions. Place each pork medallion, one at a time, in a cut-open resealable plastic bag and pound it with a meat mallet (or the bottom of a pot) until it is 1 inch (2.5 cm) thick.

2   Melt 1 Tbsp (15 mL) of the butter and the oil together in a heavy skillet over medium-high heat until the butter foams. Add the pork, seasoning lightly in the pan, and fry until golden brown, 2 to 3 minutes per side. (You may need to do this in batches.) Remove the pork to rest on a plate, and remove the fat from the pan.

3   Reduce the heat to medium and add the remaining 2 tsp (10 mL) of butter to the pan. Add the shallots and sauté until soft and golden, about 2 minutes. Stir in the cider, apple and thyme, and simmer until the liquid reduces by half. Add the cream and bring to a full simmer, then return the pork to the pan in a single layer. Simmer to warm pork through and check that it is fully cooked (since it's so thin, this will only take about 1 minute). Season to taste.

4   To serve, place 3 pork medallions and 1 potato cake on each plate and ladle the sauce overtop.

2 pork tenderloins (about 2 lb/900 g total)

1 Tbsp + 2 tsp (25 mL) butter, divided

1 Tbsp (15 mL) vegetable oil

2 Tbsp (30 mL) minced shallots

½ cup (125 mL) unsweetened apple cider

1 tart apple (such as Crispin or Ginger Crisp), peeled and diced

1 tsp (5 mL) chopped fresh thyme, leaves only

½ cup (125 mL) 35% whipping cream

Salt and pepper

Yukon Gold Potato Cakes, for serving (recipe follows)

CONTINUES

Yukon Gold Potato Cakes

1 lb (450 g) Yukon Gold potatoes (about 2 large)

1 tsp (5 mL) table salt

1 large egg

2 Tbsp (30 mL) all-purpose flour

1 Tbsp (15 mL) vegetable oil

1 Peel the potatoes and use a box grater to coarsely shred them, then squeeze out excess water and immediately stir in the salt (this prevents the potatoes from turning gray). Stir in the egg and flour, and mix evenly.

2 Heat the oil in a large nonstick skillet over medium-high heat and divide the potato mixture into 4 round pancakes. (Alternatively, you can make 1 large pancake that can be quartered once cooked.) Cook the pancakes until brown on the edges, 8 to 9 minutes. Turn over pancakes and reduce the heat to medium. Cook on the second side until golden brown and fully cooked in the middle (open one up carefully to look inside), 10 to 12 minutes. Remove to a plate and keep warm in a 225°F (110°C) oven until ready to eat.

Notes:

+ The potato cakes can be made up to a day ahead and kept wrapped in the fridge, then warmed in the oven while you cook the pork and apples.

Leg Cutlet "Tartufi"

with Truffle Honey Glaze & Grainy Mustard Sauce

These pork "truffles" are individual roasts in which a cutlet is wrapped around a sausage-like stuffing. It has a glaze of truffle honey brushed on during the last bit of cooking, making it shiny and filling the kitchen with the aroma of forest mushrooms. This is a real treat.

1   Preheat the oven to 350°F (180°C) and line the bottom of a baking pan or casserole dish with foil or parchment paper.

2   Flatten each of the cutlets in a cut-open resealable plastic bag using a meat hammer, using gentle taps to try to keep the cutlet in as round a shape as possible (since it has to wrap around a ball of filling), until they are about 7 inches (18 cm) across. Chill until ready to assemble.

3   Use your hands to blend the sausage meat, bread crumbs, pistachios, dried cherries, egg, thyme and 1 tsp (5 mL) of the truffle oil until very well combined. Shape the filling into 4 balls. Lay a cutlet overtop each "meatball" and lift it up, letting the thin cutlet wrap and cover the meatball. Use your hands to shape it — it doesn't matter if the filling isn't completely covered. Place the tartufi in the prepared dish and season lightly with salt and pepper. Roast the tartufi, uncovered, until they reach an internal temperature of 165°F (74°C), about 50 minutes. At the 40-minute mark, stir the honey and remaining ½ tsp (2 mL) of truffle oil together, brush the surface of the tartufi with the mixture and return the dish to the oven.

TARTUFI

4 large pork cutlets, from sirloin or leg (about 4 oz/120 g each)

1 lb (450 g) honey garlic sausage, casings removed

⅓ cup (80 mL) dry bread crumbs

¼ cup (60 mL) shelled pistachios

¼ cup (60 mL) dried cherries or cranberries

1 large egg

1 tsp (5 mL) chopped fresh thyme, leaves only

1½ tsp (7 mL) white or black truffle oil, divided

Salt and pepper

2 Tbsp (30 mL) honey

GRAINY MUSTARD SAUCE

2 Tbsp (30 mL) butter

1 shallot, minced

2 Tbsp (30 mL) all-purpose flour

1 cup (250 mL) 2% milk, divided

2 Tbsp (30 mL) sherry

1 Tbsp (15 mL) grainy mustard

Salt and pepper

CONTINUES

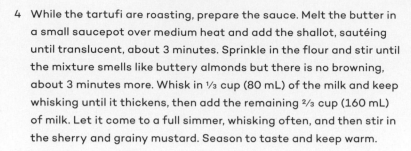

4   While the tartufi are roasting, prepare the sauce. Melt the butter in a small saucepot over medium heat and add the shallot, sautéing until translucent, about 3 minutes. Sprinkle in the flour and stir until the mixture smells like buttery almonds but there is no browning, about 3 minutes more. Whisk in ⅓ cup (80 mL) of the milk and keep whisking until it thickens, then add the remaining ⅔ cup (160 mL) of milk. Let it come to a full simmer, whisking often, and then stir in the sherry and grainy mustard. Season to taste and keep warm.

5   To serve, spoon the sauce onto each plate. Cut each tartufi into 4 wedges and arrange on top of the sauce.

Notes:

+ I make the sauce and prepare the meat a couple of hours before the guests arrive, then roast the tartufi when we need them and simply reheat the sauce. Where truffle products used to be hard to find, they are now available in most supermarkets or in your local gourmet shop. If you can't get truffle oil, add a shot of brandy or orange liqueur to the honey before glazing the pork.

Pork Schnitzel

Schnitzel... The word evokes images of golden, crisp, yet juicy pork as big as, wait, *bigger than* the plate—like Persian carpets hanging over the side of the serving dish. They can be dressed with simple lemon or extravagant sauces and toppings. But at the end of the day, it's all about the schnitzel. Shall we?

2 lb (900 g) boneless pork loin roast

Salt and pepper

2 cups (500 mL) all-purpose flour

4 large eggs, lightly whisked, for brushing

2 cups (500 mL) dry bread crumbs

Vegetable oil, for frying

3 lemons, cut in wedges with center pith and seeds removed

CHOPS AND STEAKS

1   Remove the visible layer of silver skin on the top side of the loin (see page 21 for tips). Slice the meat into 6 equal portions, about 1 inch (2.5 cm) thick. Place the cutlets, one at a time, inside a large cut-open resealable plastic bag. Pound with the flat side of a meat tenderizer until it doubles in width, with a thickness of about ¼ inch (6 mm). Repeat with the remaining cutlets.

2   Season each of the cutlets with salt and pepper, and set up a dredging station with 3 bowls, one each for the flour, egg and bread crumbs.

3   Heat about ½ inch (1 cm) of vegetable oil in a heavy-bottomed skillet over medium-high heat to 325°F (160°C) and line a baking sheet with a wire cooling rack. Use tongs to dredge the cutlets one at a time in the flour, knocking off any excess, then fully dip into the egg and, finally, into the bread crumbs to lightly coat the meat.

4   Add a single schnitzel to the oil. You can use kitchen tongs to move it around and turn it over once it is golden brown, about 90 seconds. Once both sides have browned and the schnitzel is starting to crisp, remove it to the rack set on the baking sheet to drain off any excess oil. You may have to raise or lower the heat to maintain the oil temperature at 325°F (160°C). Once you have cooked all the schnitzels, they can be reheated in a 350°F (180°C) oven for 5 to 7 minutes.

5   Serve the schnitzels on a platter that has been warmed in the oven, or plate individually with a wedge of lemon on the side or consider the classic variations on pages 180–81.

CONTINUES

Notes:

+   The basic breading method is called "dry-wet-dry": flour-egg wash-bread crumbs is the norm, but you could make substitutions, such as cornstarch instead of flour. Knock or drip off the excess from each station before dipping in the next to avoid bare spots in the breading.

Topping Variations

Classic

```
12 anchovy fillets, cut in half
   lengthwise
2 Tbsp (30 mL) capers
```

Arrange 2 anchovy slices on each schnitzel in an "X" pattern and dot with the capers.

Hammer Max

```
6 slices Black Forest ham
6 slices Emmental cheese
6 large eggs
1 Tbsp (15 mL) butter
```

Cover each schnitzel with a ham slice, topped by a cheese slice, and then warm in a 350°F (180°C) oven until the cheese has melted. While the schnitzels are in the oven, fry the eggs in the butter over medium heat for about 4 minutes, then flip and cook until over-easy, about 1 minute more. Gently place 1 egg on each schnitzel before serving.

Hunter

Pizzaiolo

⅓ lb (225 g) cremini mushrooms, sliced

1 shallot, minced

1 Tbsp (15 mL) butter

1 tsp (5 mL) chopped fresh thyme, leaves
only

1 Tbsp (15 mL) brandy

1 cup (250 mL) 35% whipping cream

Salt and pepper

Sauté the mushrooms and shallot in the butter
over medium-high heat until any liquid has
evaporated, about 3 minutes. Stir in the thyme,
then add the brandy and simmer for 1 minute.
Stir in the cream and simmer until the sauce
has reduced enough to coat the back of a
spoon, about 5 minutes. Season to taste and
spoon over the schnitzels.

1 cup (250 mL) diced fresh mozzarella
(bocconcini)

1 cup (250 mL) shredded radicchio

1 cup (250 mL) quartered marinated artichoke hearts

12 cherry tomatoes, quartered

12 pitted black olives

12 fresh basil leaves

1 Tbsp (15 mL) red wine vinegar

Salt and pepper

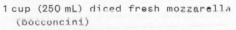

Toss the mozzarella, radicchio, artichokes,
tomatoes, olives, basil and vinegar together in
a bowl, season to taste and spoon over the
schnitzels.

Pan Fried Tenderloin Medallions

in Marsala Sauce

This tenderloin recipe involves a quick pan-fry to crisp the surface and cook the meat, and then the sauce is made in the same pan, getting its robust character from the marsala and a nugget of butter to make it rich and thick. This dish may sound "cheffy," but it is easy to make and the technique can be applied to other sear-and-sauce preparations.

1 pork tenderloin (about 1 lb/450 g)

Salt and pepper

3 Tbsp (45 mL) cornstarch, divided

1 Tbsp (15 mL) olive oil

1 shallot, minced

1 tsp (5 mL) chopped fresh thyme, leaves only

¼ cup (60 mL) dry marsala wine

¾ cup (175 mL) chicken or beef stock, divided

1 tsp (5 mL) butter

1 Remove the silver skin from the tenderloin (see page 21 for tips), and cut into 6 equal slices. Gently flatten the pork by placing each piece in a cut-open resealable plastic bag and lightly pounding it with a meat mallet (or the bottom of a pot) until it is about 1 inch (2.5 cm) thick.

2 Season the pork lightly with salt and pepper, then toss in a bowl with 2 Tbsp (30 mL) of the cornstarch until coated. Remove to a plate, shaking off any excess cornstarch.

3 Heat the oil in a heavy-bottomed skillet over medium high heat and cook the pork until it develops a golden crust, about 3 minutes per side. Transfer to a plate while preparing the sauce.

4 Reduce the heat to medium, add the shallot and thyme to the pan and stir for 1 minute to soften the shallot. Deglaze the pan with the marsala wine, stirring with a wooden spoon to pull up any bits stuck to the pan, then add ½ cup (125 mL) of the stock and bring to a simmer. Cook until reduced by one-third, 3 to 4 minutes. Whisk the remaining 1 Tbsp (15 mL) of cornstarch into the remaining ¼ cup (60 mL) of stock and add to the pan. Return the pork to the pan to reheat in the sauce, turning so it is fully glazed, and then stir in the butter until fully blended. Season to taste with salt and pepper.

5 To serve, place 3 pork slices on each plate and spoon the sauce overtop, serving any extra on the side. This dish is great with potatoes, steamed green vegetables and carrots.

Notes:

+ Be sure to use dry, not sweet, marsala in this recipe, or the sauce will be reminiscent of tiramisu.

Mild Yellow Thai Curry Tenderloin

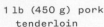

- 1 lb (450 g) pork tenderloin
- 1 Tbsp (15 mL) vegetable oil
- ½ medium onion, diced
- 3 Tbsp (45 mL) yellow curry paste
- 1 cup (250 mL) full-fat coconut milk
- 2 small carrots, peeled and diced
- ½ lb (225 g) green beans, cut in 1-inch (2.5 cm) pieces (about 2 cups/500 mL)
- 1 small zucchini, diced (about 1 cup/250 mL)
- 1 Roma tomato, diced
- Salt and pepper
- 4 cups (1 L) cooked jasmine rice, for serving
- Chopped roasted peanuts and chopped fresh cilantro, for serving

If you want to try new taste sensations but are not keen on fiery hot chilies, this dish has plenty of flavor from the spice mix, without the heat. You can always serve hot sauce on the side for those who want the kick of intense chili heat, or try the same recipe with either red or green Thai curry paste (they are hot!).

1 Trim the silver skin from the tenderloin (see page 21 for tips) and dice the meat into 1-inch (2.5 cm) pieces.

2 Heat the oil in a heavy-bottomed skillet over medium-high heat and add the onion and curry paste, sautéing until the curry paste aromas "wake up," about 1 minute. Stir in the coconut milk and simmer until the onions are soft, about 5 minutes. Stir in the pork, followed by the carrots, beans and zucchini, and simmer until the vegetables are tender and the pork is cooked through, about 10 minutes. Stir in the tomato to warm them through and season to taste.

3 Serve over cooked jasmine rice and top with the roasted peanuts and cilantro.

Notes:

+ Thai curry paste is available at Asian grocery stores, but if you can't find it, substitute 2 Tbsp (30 mL) yellow curry powder and the zest of a lime to achieve a similar flavor.

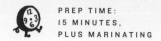

Grilled Citrus Mojo Marinated Tenderloin

My chef friend Oswaldo from Cuba used to cook for the big army bosses when he served and told me how he made pork in a bitter orange–olive oil marinade, a favorite recipe of a certain bearded historical character. The combination of citrus, garlic and herbs is ideal for the beach and hot summer weather. And don't be cheap with the rum in that mojito!

1 pork tenderloin (about 1 lb/450 g)

1 seedless orange, thinly sliced

2 limes, thinly sliced

2 cloves garlic, crushed

2 green onions, chopped

2 Tbsp (30 mL) olive oil

1 tsp (5 mL) dried oregano

Salt and pepper

Orange and lime slices, for garnish

---

1 Butterfly the pork (see how on page 22) and trim the silver skin.

2 Combine the orange slices, lime slices, garlic, green onions, oil and oregano in a shallow dish and add the pork, turning a few times to coat. Cover and chill in the fridge for at least 1 hour or overnight. (The longer the meat sits in the marinade, the more intense the flavors will be once cooked.)

3 Preheat the grill to high. Remove the pork from the marinade and season with salt and pepper. Grill the pork with the lid closed until it reaches an internal temperature of 145°F (63°C), 3 to 4 minutes per side. Remove to rest on a cutting board for 3 minutes before slicing.

4 To serve, slice across the grain (not lengthwise) into strips and serve with fresh orange and lime slices, grilled bread and a tomato salad. You can also serve hot sauce on the side, if desired (but Oswaldo would not!).

Notes:

+ The quick cook time of the butterflied tenderloin means it doesn't require any basting, but if you use the same preparation for thick-cut chops, you can baste with the marinade as they cook to an internal temperature of 145°F (63°C).

 YIELD: 4 SERVINGS

 PREP TIME:
25 MINUTES,
PLUS CHILLING

COOK TIME:
25 MINUTES

Grilled Garlic Lemon Tenderloin

with Shopska Salad

188

2 pork tenderloins (about
  2 lb/900 g total)

2 Tbsp (30 mL) olive oil

2 cloves garlic, minced

2 tsp (5 mL) dried oregano

1 tsp (5 mL) finely grated
  lemon zest

1 tsp (5 mL) fine salt

1 tsp (5 mL) ground black
  pepper

SALAD

1 red bell pepper, seeded
  and diced

1 yellow bell pepper,
  seeded and diced

1 English cucumber, diced

3 plum tomatoes, cored
  and chopped

1 small red onion, finely
  diced

3 Tbsp (45 mL) chopped
  fresh Italian parsley

3 Tbsp (45 mL) olive oil

1 Tbsp (15 mL) red wine
  vinegar

Salt and pepper

3 oz (90 g) crumbled feta
  cheese (about
  ½ cup/125 mL)

I've eaten Greek salad many times but came across Shopska, from the Bulgarian kitchen, while on a trip to Bulgaria's capital city, Sofia. The salad has a similar preparation to Greek salad, minus the olives. It's ideal for summer grilling outdoors.

1 Trim the silver skin from the pork (see page 21 for tips). Stir the olive oil with the garlic, oregano, lemon zest, salt and pepper, and rub the mixture over the pork. Cover and chill for 1 hour.

2 For the salad, toss together the bell peppers, cucumber, tomatoes, onion, parsley, oil and vinegar, and then season to taste. Sprinkle the top of the salad with the crumbled feta just before serving. The salad can be prepared up to 4 hours ahead of time.

3 Preheat the grill to medium-high, and remove the pork from the marinade. Grill the pork, with the grill lid closed, until it reaches an internal temperature of 145°F (63°C), 10 to 12 minutes per side. Remove to rest on a cutting board for 5 minutes. Slice each tenderloin across the grain into 6 slices and serve with the shopska salad. Use some of the juices from the salad to dress the sliced tenderloin.

YIELD: 6 SERVINGS
AS AN APPETIZER

PREP TIME:
15 MINUTES,
PLUS MARINATING

COOK TIME:
20 MINUTES

Grilled Korean Style Belly

Korean barbecue is something I've enjoyed at restaurants for years, so I finally decided to bring it home! I marinate the sliced belly overnight, and then grill it as dinner guests arrive. It gets sliced into bite-sized pieces that can be picked up with a small fork or toothpick.

---

1 Make cuts through the skin of the pork (a box cutter is the best tool for this) at 1-inch (2.5 cm) intervals. Cut the pork into ¼-inch (6 mm) thick slices—you should get between 8 and 12 slices, depending on the size of the pork belly.

2 Stir together the ketchup, soy sauce, Worcestershire, ginger, garlic and sesame oil in a shallow dish and then add the pork. Toss and massage thoroughly to get the marinade onto every bit of the meat's surface. Cover and chill for 2 hours or overnight.

3 Preheat the grill to medium-high (reduce the heat to medium, if needed, to avoid flare-ups) and cook the pork, turning every 4 minutes and putting the lid on the grill after each turn, until the outside of the slices get dark brown and crispy, and the meat is cooked through (you can check by taking a small slice to test), about 16 minutes. Transfer the pork to a cutting board and sprinkle with the toasted sesame seeds.

4 To serve, cut into small portions and serve with hot sauce and lemon wedges.

1 lb (450 g) skin-on fresh pork belly

2 Tbsp (30 mL) ketchup

1 Tbsp (15 mL) soy sauce

8-10 dashes Worcestershire sauce

1 Tbsp (15 mL) finely minced ginger

2 cloves garlic, minced

1 tsp (5 mL) sesame oil

1 Tbsp (15 ml) toasted sesame seeds

Hot sauce and lemon wedges, for serving

CHOPS AND STEAKS

191

Notes:

+ This dish can be turned into more substantial appetizers by making lettuce wraps with sliced cucumbers,

hot sauce and kimchi (spicy Korean sauerkraut). You can buy good-quality kimchi to serve on the side like pickles.

+ If you buy pre-sliced pork belly, you can still make the cuts just through the skin to allow it to absorb the marinade better.

"Garage" Chops

with Caper Dressing

LIVING HIGH OFF THE HOG

CAPER DRESSING

3 Tbsp (45 mL) capers, drained and roughly chopped

3 Tbsp (45 mL) chopped fresh Italian parsley

2 Tbsp (30 mL) fresh lemon juice

2 Tbsp (30 mL) finely sliced green onions

1 Tbsp (15 mL) caper brine (from the jar)

1 Tbsp (15 mL) grainy mustard

3 dashes hot sauce

3 dashes Worcestershire sauce

¼ cup (60 mL) olive oil

1 hard-boiled large egg

Salt and pepper

CHOPS

3 large eggs

⅓ cup (80 mL) finely grated Parmigiano-Reggiano cheese

3 Tbsp (45 mL) vegetable oil

2 lb (900 g) bone-in pork chops (about 8 chops)

Salt and pepper

I have heard the story so many times: someone's father makes homemade sausage with his friends and they end up hanging out in the garage, frying sausage and chops in an electric skillet, tasting homemade wine and solving the world's problems. The old guys sit around on beat-up chairs, eating with their hands. I used to have to work every Saturday when I was a chef, so I dreamed of someday having the spare time on the weekend to enjoy Garage Chops.

1 For the caper dressing, whisk the capers, parsley, lemon juice, green onions, caper brine, grainy mustard, hot sauce and Worcestershire sauce in a small bowl until well-combined. Drizzle in the olive oil in a thin stream while whisking constantly, until the oil is incorporated. Use the coarse side of a box grater to grate the hard-boiled egg into the sauce, season to taste and chill until ready to serve.

2 Preheat the oven to 300°F (150°C). Line a baking sheet with foil or parchment paper and put a cooling rack overtop.

3 In a shallow dish, use a fork to stir together the eggs and cheese. Heat the oil in a heavy-bottomed skillet or a large electric griddle over medium-high heat. Season the chops with the salt and pepper. Use tongs to dip the chops in the egg mixture, shaking off any excess, and carefully place in the pan, dropping the chops in away from you and leaving 1 inch (2.5 cm) between each chop. (You may have to do this in batches.) Fry until the chops are firm to the touch and golden brown, and reach an internal temperature of 145°F (63°C), about 4 minutes per side. Transfer the cooked chops to the baking sheet to keep warm in the oven while finishing the remaining chops.

4 Serve warm with the caper dressing. Of course, if you're in the house, feel free to use cutlery, otherwise, if you're in the garage, you might be holding these in a paper napkin!

Notes:

+ This sauce is sharp and tangy, and will keep for 3 days in the fridge. You can easily adapt it with more or less of an ingredient and switch up the herbs according to what's in the garden or fridge, such as chives or mint. The dressing is also excellent on cold roast pork in a sandwich.

Pumpernickel Stuffed Pork Chops

with Pear Gingersnap Sauce

This recipe is sure to impress, and the effort is well worth the result. The golden brown chops are filled with a dark ruby jewel of a pumpernickel and cranberry stuffing, and the gravy is rich with splendid pear and gingersnap aromas—man, it smells like Christmas in here!

1 For the stuffing, pulse one-quarter of the sliced onion (about ½ cup/125 mL) with the celery in a food processor. Add the pumpernickel and cranberries, and pulse until quite finely chopped. Transfer to a bowl and stir in ¼ cup (60 mL) of the white wine along with the thyme, mustard, salt and pepper (1, next page). Stir well to break mixture down and soften to almost a paste consistency. Spoon stuffing into a large disposable piping bag (no tip needed). If you don't have a piping bag, use a resealable plastic bag with one corner cut off.

2 To prepare the chops, insert the tip of a paring knife into the base of the chop, close to the bottom of the rib bone. Wiggle the knife from one side of the chop to the other, in an arc, to create a pocket for the stuffing—try not to cut through the chop (2, next page). Insert the tip of the piping bag into the pocket and insert as much stuffing as you can (the chop will swell). Repeat with the remaining chops until all of the stuffing has been used (3, next page). Chill until ready to cook.

3 Preheat the oven to 350°F (180°C).

4 Heat a large ovenproof skillet over medium-high heat and add the butter and oil. Once the butter foams and then the foaming subsides, drop in the chops, seasoning lightly on each side when in the pan, and flipping over once browned, about 4 minutes per side. Remove the chops from the pan and reduce the heat to medium. Add the remaining sliced onion and the pear, and toss to coat in the butter. Arrange the chops on top of the onion-pear mixture and roast in the oven, uncovered, until the chops reach an internal temperature of 145°F (63°C), about 30 minutes.

STUFFING

1 medium onion, sliced

½ stalk celery, coarsely chopped

2 cups (500 mL) roughly diced day-old pumpernickel bread

½ cup (125 mL) fresh or thawed frozen cranberries

½ cup (125 mL) dry white wine, divided

1 tsp (5 mL) chopped fresh thyme, leaves only

1 tsp (5 mL) grainy mustard

½ tsp (2 mL) fine salt, plus extra for seasoning

¼ tsp (1 mL) ground black pepper, plus extra for seasoning

4 (8 oz/260 g) bone-in center cut loin chops

SAUCE

1 Tbsp (15 mL) butter

1 Tbsp (15 mL) vegetable oil

1 Bartlett pear, unpeeled, cored and cut in 8 wedges

1 cup (250 mL) chicken stock

½ cup (125 mL) gingersnap crumbs

CONTINUES

1.

2.

3.

5 Transfer the pan from the oven to the stove over medium heat, being careful of the pan's hot handles, and place the chops on a cutting board to rest. Add the remaining ¼ cup (60 mL) of white wine to the pan, stirring with a wooden spoon and gently pulling up any onion or pear bits that have stuck to the bottom, until the liquid reaches a simmer. Stir in the chicken stock and return to a simmer. Sprinkle in the gingersnap crumbs and stir until the sauce thickens and becomes glossy—this only takes a minute. Season to taste and serve the chops over the sauce.

Notes:

+ This dish was inspired by German *sauerbraten*, which uses gingersnap cookies to thicken its vinegar sauce. The sweetness of the cookie addition is very subtle— it's the spices that really shine through. Use crispy, thin gingersnaps for this recipe, not chewy, molasses-heavy ones.

Pojarski Chops with Mushroom Cream

Pojarski is a dish in which the meat from the chop is taken off the bone, diced and minced to a fine mousse with cream. It is then shaped to look like a chop and breaded. The bone is put back in place, and the whole thing is cooked and served with a rich sauce. I first made this dish in cooking school and did not understand the history—the recipe was developed before people had food processors or meat grinders, and the idea was to prepare a piece of meat in the most tender way possible. Of course, in modern times, this can look like over-processed factory food. A few years ago, I ate this same dish at a classical Russian restaurant in Moscow and finally appreciated it in its full glory. It only took me 30 years after cooking school... bit of a slow learner, I guess.

1   Soak the day-old white bread in the milk for 15 minutes, stirring once or twice.

2   Meanwhile, cut the pork rack into individual bones, cutting away as much meat and trim from the bones as possible. Chill for 10 minutes. Reserve the bones. Dice the meat (including the fat) and place in a food processor along with any trim from the bones. Add the fine salt and process to a fine paste. Add the egg, mustard and milk-soaked bread, then pulse again until smooth. Cover and refrigerate for 30 minutes.

3   Divide the meat mixture into 4 equal portions and shape into "chops"—the shape and diameter of a thick-cut pork chop. Place the panettone cubes in a flat dish and press the "chops" into the cubes, pressing and filling in any gaps with your hands. Now insert a reserved bone into each portion so it really looks like a chop.

4   Preheat the oven to 350°F (180°C) and line a baking sheet with parchment paper. Gently lay the 4 chops on the tray and roast minutes until the egg bread is golden and the internal temperature of the meat is 155°F (68°C), 35 to 40 minutes.

1½ cups (375 mL) diced day-old white bread (without crust)

½ cup (125 mL) 2% milk

3 lb (1.4 kg) pork rack (at least 4 bones, frenched)

1 tsp (5 mL) fine salt

1 large egg

1 Tbsp (15 mL) Dijon mustard

4 cups (1 L) finely diced (¼–½ inch/6 mm–1 cm) panettone or egg bread (without crust), lightly toasted

1 Tbsp (15 mL) butter

½ lb (225 g) cremini mushrooms, quartered

1 small shallot, diced

¾ cup (175 mL) 35% whipping cream

2 Tbsp (30 mL) brandy

Salt and pepper

CONTINUES

5   While the chops cook, heat a saucepot over medium-high heat and melt the butter. Add the mushrooms and shallot, and sauté until any liquid has evaporated from the pan, about 8 minutes. Add the cream and brandy, reduce the heat and simmer until the sauce is thick enough that it coats the back of a spoon, about 4 minutes. Season to taste.

6   Once the chops are cooked, remove from the oven and let rest for 5 minutes. Serve the warm chops over the cream sauce.

Notes:

+   "Frenched" means the bones are exposed, scraped clean of any meat or fat. Ask your butcher for a pork rack and cut it into chops yourself to ensure you get the right size and one bone per person.

+   Toast the diced panettone or egg bread for 10 minutes in a 350°F (180°C) oven to crisp before using.

+   Because you are grinding your own meat from a chop, you do not have to cook it to 165°F (74°C) like you would with store-bought ground meat.

Butt Chops Puttanesca

YIELD: 4 SERVINGS

PREP TIME:
15 MINUTES

COOK TIME:
ABOUT 1 HOUR,
15 MINUTES

The well-known Italian pasta dish gives this sauce its name. It has intense flavors of garlic, chilies, olives, capers and anchovies in a tomato sauce. The long, slow cooking of the shoulder (butt) chops in this brazen sauce will make you blush, but only because you can't get over how delicious it is.

1 Heat the oil in a large skillet over medium-high heat. Season the chops and sear until golden brown, about 3 minutes per side, and then transfer to a plate.

2 Reduce the heat to medium, add the onion and celery, and sauté until the onion is translucent, about 5 minutes. Stir in the garlic, anchovy paste and chili flakes, and cook for 1 minute more. Add the wine and tomatoes, and bring to a simmer. Add the chops back into the sauce, cover and gently simmer (lowering the heat, if needed) until fork-tender, about 1½ hours. Stir in the olives, parsley and capers. Season to taste and serve over cooked pasta.

2 tsp (10 mL) vegetable oil

Salt and pepper

4 fresh boneless butt chops (about 2 lb/900 g total)

½ medium onion, diced

1 stalk celery, diced

1 clove garlic, minced

2 tsp (10 mL) anchovy paste

2 tsp (10 mL) dried chili flakes

½ cup (125 mL) dry white wine

1 can (28 oz/796 mL) crushed tomatoes

½ cup (125 mL) stuffed green olives

2 Tbsp (30 mL) chopped fresh Italian parsley

1 Tbsp (15 mL) drained capers

4 cups cooked short pasta, such as rigatoni or penne

Notes:

+   Loin chops are too lean for long braising and might dry out, so the butt chops will be juicy and tender.

 YIELD: 4 SERVINGS

 PREP TIME:
10 MINUTES,
PLUS CHILLING

 COOK TIME:
25 MINUTES

Boneless Loin Chops in BBQ Rub

with Chimichurri

Chimichurri is a sauce that comes from Argentina, where they take grilled meat very seriously. Although this sauce usually goes on beef, it goes wonderfully with grilled pork chops because the smoky meat takes on the pungent flavor of the garlic-herb paste. I make this in batches throughout the summer and keep it in a covered dish in the fridge for up to 1 week.

---

1   Cover the chops with the BBQ rub, massaging it in with your hands, and chill for 1 hour.

2   For the chimichurri, use a blender or food processor to puree the olive oil, parsley, chives, basil, red wine vinegar, thyme, garlic, oregano, salt and pepper until finely chopped. This can be prepared up to 1 week ahead and stored in the fridge.

3   Preheat the grill to medium and grill the chops, with the lid on, until they reach an internal temperature of 145°F (63°C), about 12 minutes per side. Remove the chops to a cutting board to rest for 5 minutes.

4   To serve, slice each chop into 5 pieces on an angle and fan them out on the plate. Dollop some chimichurri on top, plus include more on the side.

4   thick-cut boneless loin chops (8-10 oz/ 225-280 g each)
3   Tbsp (45 mL) Basic BBQ Rub (page 267)

CHIMICHURRI

¾ cup (175 mL) olive oil
¾ cup (175 mL) loosely packed fresh Italian parsley leaves
½ cup (125 mL) chopped fresh chives
½ cup (125 mL) fresh basil leaves
2 Tbsp (30 mL) red wine vinegar
1 Tbsp (15 mL) fresh thyme leaves
3 cloves garlic, crushed
2 tsp (10 mL) dried oregano
1 tsp (5 mL) fine salt
1 tsp (5 ml) ground black pepper

Notes:

+ Grilled meats like this need plenty of vegetables on the side. Serve this dish with tomato slices, grilled zucchini, bean salad and a bottle of Malbec (OK, while the wine is not really a salad, it *is* made from fruit).

YIELD: 4 SERVINGS

PREP TIME:
10 MINUTES,
PLUS MARINATING

COOK TIME:
25 MINUTES

Grilled Shoulder Steaks

in Onion Beer Marinade with Apricot Vinegar Glaze

Not only do onions add great flavor to many pork dishes, but their natural enzymes can also help tenderize tougher cuts of meat. These steaks will come off the grill juicy and full of lip-smacking goodness, with the little bit of char from the grill balanced by the sweet and sour apricot glaze.

4 pork shoulder blade or capicola steaks (about 2 lb/900 g total)

1 medium onion, peeled and quartered

1 cup (250 mL) cold beer (see note)

2 tsp (10 mL) chopped fresh thyme, leaves only

Salt and pepper

3 Tbsp (45 mL) apricot jam

2 Tbsp (30 mL) white wine vinegar

205

1 Place the steaks in a large flat dish. Use a food processor or immersion blender to puree the onion, beer and thyme, and pour the mixture over the steaks, stirring it around to coat the meat fully. Cover and chill for at least 1 hour, or up to 12 hours. The longer you marinate the steaks, the more pronounced the onion flavor will be.

2 Preheat the grill to medium-high. Remove the steaks from the marinade, wipe off any excess onion and season with salt and pepper. Grill the steaks, turning once, until they reach an internal temperature of 145°F (63°C), about 10 minutes per side.

3 While the steaks are grilling, stir the apricot jam and vinegar together. Brush the mixture onto both sides of the steaks during their last few minutes on the grill.

4 Serve with potato salad, greens and asparagus. This dish is also great served with ice-cold beer or a glass of Riesling.

Notes:

+ You can choose your favorite local craft beer to add color or bitter hop character. I like a hoppy IPA, with its thyme and citrus aromas; the bitterness is tempered by the sweet apricot glaze. While shoulder cuts are most often eaten after a long, slow braise, these steaks are tender and juicy from the onion marinade and a quick sear on the hot grill, which caramelizes the surface but does not dry out the meat.

+ Generally, the following three recipes (Grilled T-Bones in Soy Whiskey Marinade; Grilled Loin Chops in Garlic Dijon Marinade with Jalapeño BBQ Sauce; and Pan Roasted T-Bones in Lemon Parm Glaze) are interchangeable when it comes to chop, marinade and sauce. The cooking times will vary, but each cut of meat should be heated to an internal temperature of 145°F (63°C).

YIELD: 4 SERVINGS

PREP TIME:
10 MINUTES,
PLUS MARINATING

COOK TIME:
25 MINUTES

Grilled T-Bones

in Soy Whiskey Marinade

¼ cup (60 mL) orange
   juice

3 Tbsp (45 mL) soy sauce

2 Tbsp (30 mL) rye whiskey

1-inch (2.5 cm) piece
   fresh ginger, unpeeled
   and sliced

1 Tbsp (15 mL) packed
   light brown sugar

1 garlic clove, crushed

1 whole star anise

4 thick-cut pork T-bone
   chops (8-10 oz/
   225-280 g each)

Like a teriyaki-glazed chop, these T-bones will come off the grill with a mahogany glaze full of flavor and great aromas of citrus and ginger. The soy and sugar act like a brine, keeping the meat juicy, and the shot of whiskey brings out the light hint of licorice from the star anise.

———————

1   Whisk the orange juice, soy sauce, whiskey, ginger, brown sugar, garlic and star anise in a large flat dish. Add the chops and turn them over to coat fully in the marinade. Cover and chill, turning over once or twice, for at least 1 hour or overnight. The longer the chops marinate, the more pronounced the flavor will be.

2   Preheat the grill to medium and remove the meat from the marinade, shaking off any excess. Grill until the chops are dark brown in color, and have reached an internal temperature of 145°F (63°C), about 12 minutes per side. You can baste with the marinade for the first half of the cooking process to develop a shine and keep the meat moist.

3   Serve with coleslaw and grilled vegetables.

Notes:

+   In terms of a wine pairing, red wine does not like soy sauce (it makes it taste astringent), so choose a sparkling rosé, gewürztraminer or Belgian witbier to go with this dish.

Grilled Loin Chops in Garlic Dijon Marinade

with Jalapeño BBQ Sauce

Although this is quite a simple preparation, these thick-cut single-bone chops will take on the garlic marinade and then get a shellacking of spicy, smoky, sweet glaze. This dish will elicit a compliment like "Now, that's a pork chop!" and you can take full credit.

1   Whisk the mustard, garlic, thyme and olive oil in a large flat dish. Add in the chops and turn them over to fully coat. Cover and chill for at least 1 hour, or up to 1 day ahead.

2   Preheat the grill to medium and remove the chops from the marinade, shaking off any excess. Season the chops with salt and pepper. Grill until the chops have reached an internal temperature of 145°F (63°C), about 10 minutes per side.

3   While the chops are grilling, stir the BBQ sauce with the minced jalapeños and jalapeño pickle juice. Brush over both sides of the chops for the last few minutes of cooking.

4   Remove the chops to rest for 5 minutes before serving with the cucumber salad.

2 Tbsp (30 mL) Dijon mustard

2 cloves garlic, minced

1 Tbsp (15 mL) chopped fresh thyme, leaves only

1 Tbsp (15 mL) olive oil

4 thick-cut bone-in rib chops (8–10 oz/ 225–280 g each)

Salt and pepper

¼ cup (60 mL) prepared BBQ sauce or Lipstick on a Pig BBQ Sauce (page 270)

2 Tbsp (30 mL) minced pickled jalapeño peppers

2 Tbsp (30 mL) jalapeño pickle juice (from the jar)

Cool Creamy Cucumber Salad, for serving (page 212)

209

CHOPS AND STEAKS

Notes:

+   Jalapeño pickle juice can be used in place of vinegar to flavor marinades or even salad dressings. If you don't want the jalapeño heat, dill pickle juice also works well.

+   There are a lot of great BBQ sauces available in grocery stores, but I find many of them are too sweet and too thick, so I thin them out with vinegar for balance. For more of my thoughts on prepared BBQ sauces, check out page 269.

Pan Roasted T-Bones

in Lemon Parm Glaze

1 Tbsp (15 mL) vegetable oil

4 thick-cut pork T-Bone chops (8-10 oz/225-280 g each)

Salt and pepper

1 lemon

¼ cup (60 mL) mayonnaise

3 Tbsp (45 mL) freshly grated Parmigiano-Reggiano cheese

Crispy Roasted Potatoes, for serving (page 213)

This is a mighty cut, one that should be the center of attention on the plate, so much so that I will serve all my vegetables on the side. Behold! The T-bone! Yes, that will do just fine, thanks.

1 Preheat the oven to 350°F (180°C).

2 Heat the oil in a large heavy-bottomed skillet over medium-high heat. Working with 2 chops at a time, sear both sides of the chops, seasoning them as they go into the pan, until they are a golden brown, about 4 minutes per side. Remove the chops from the pan and the skillet from the heat.

3 Juice the lemon, saving the rind. Whisk the lemon juice with the mayonnaise and cheese until smooth. Slice the lemon rind into thin slices and lay in a single layer in the cooled skillet. Return the chops to the pan and slather with the lemon-mayonnaise mixture.

4 Put the skillet in the oven until the internal temperature of the chops is 145°F (63°C), about 10 minutes. Rest the chops in the pan on a cooling rack for 5 minutes before serving with roasted potatoes and a green salad.

Notes:

+ T-bone chops are from the back end of the loin and have two muscles that are separated by the back bone: the tenderloin and the eye of the loin. Many people prefer meat cooked on the bone, and it will be juiciest next to the bone, so that is where you should insert your probe thermometer to check the temperature.

Cool Creamy Cucumber Salad

½ cup (125 mL) plain yogurt (3.25% MF)

¼ cup (60 mL) chopped fresh dill

¼ cup (60 mL) chopped green onion

Juice of ½ lemon

1 tsp (5 mL) fine salt

1 English cucumber, diced

Shelled roasted pumpkin seeds, for sprinkling

You'll be adding this salad to meats and slathering it on sandwiches. It's just a great, fresh, crisp cucumber taste in the slightly sour dill yogurt.

1 In a large bowl, whisk the yogurt, dill, green onion, lemon juice and salt until smooth. Stir in the cucumber and chill until ready to serve. Serve topped with a sprinkling of pumpkin seeds.

Crispy Roasted Potatoes

These are also known in my kitchen as "Sunday Roast Potatoes." They get all golden and crispy from a turn in the hot oven, producing a crunch on the outside with a creamy, fluffy inside.

———————

1 Preheat the oven to 350°F (180°C).

2 Scrub, peel and cut the potatoes into 1½-inch (4 cm) chunks. Place the potatoes in a large pot filled with salted cold water. Bring to a boil over high heat, then reduce to medium heat and simmer until they are almost fully cooked but still quite firm (inserting a paring knife to test will meet with some resistance), about 5 minutes. Drain in a colander and let dry for 1 minute.

3 Heat the oil in a large ovenproof sauté pan over medium-high heat, add the drained potatoes and season lightly. Stir to coat the potatoes evenly with the oil, cooking for 2 to 3 minutes to start them browning, then transfer the pan to the oven. Bake, uncovered and stirring occasionally, until golden brown and crispy, about 25 minutes.

4 medium Yukon Gold or russet potatoes

2 Tbsp (30 mL) vegetable oil

Salt and pepper

213

Notes:

+ Potatoes tend to get crispier edges when they are all cut to the same size but have a slightly irregular shape. Parboiling the potatoes until the centers are still firm but the outer edges are almost crumbling is what gives the soft yet crispy texture. Be sure to leave them in the hot oven long enough to develop that golden brown crust.

ROASTS AND BIG CUTS

MODEL: 285   **MANUFACTURER:** Globe   **YEAR:** 1965

NOTES: Slicers are like old cars—you can tell the vintage by the overall shape and any add-ons. The large size and chrome detailing on this slicer remind me of the Chevy that my brother, Mark, had as a grease-ball teenager.

Y
U
M
M

Roast Pork Loin

with Maple Beer Glaze

This is a really delicious roast for a dinner party, and the recipe can be easily cut in half to serve four. The loin is a lean, easy-to-carve roast, and the glaze brings a complexity of flavor without fussy technique. Teach this one to kids heading off to live independently for college or work; think of it as a survival skill.

1 Preheat the oven to 350°F (180°C).

2 Season the pork with salt and pepper. Place the sliced lemons and garlic in a roasting pan, then place the pork on top. Roast uncovered for 75–90 minutes, to an internal temperature of 145°F (63°C), then remove it to a cutting board to rest for 5 minutes.

3 While the roast is cooking, place the beer, stock, maple syrup, shallots and thyme in a saucepot and simmer over medium heat until the mixture has reduced to 2 cups (500 mL), about 25 minutes. When the roast is ready, whisk the cubed, chilled butter into the reduced glaze to thicken it slightly. Season with salt and pepper to taste.

4 To serve, carve the roast into ½-inch (1 cm) slices and serve smothered in the maple beer glaze.

ROAST

4 lb (1.8 kg) fresh pork loin

Salt and pepper

2 lemons, each sliced in 8 rounds

2 cloves garlic, sliced

GLAZE

2 cups (500 mL) dark beer

2 cups (500 mL) chicken stock

½ cup (125 mL) pure maple syrup

2 shallots, minced

2 tsp (10 mL) chopped fresh thyme, leaves only

3 Tbsp (45 mL) butter, cubed and kept chilled

Salt and pepper

217

Notes:

+ Pork loin is a really common roast but is often overcooked and dry because it is very lean and cooks quickly. You'll have success in the kitchen by training yourself to use a thermometer to get the finished temperature right and by serving full-flavored sauces that complement the roast, like this Maple Beer Glaze. For a nice weekend brunch, serve leftover slices warmed in the sauce with pancakes and eggs.

Pork Loin Pinwheel Roast

Sometimes you want to put in the effort to impress—this stuffed rolled loin will show off your culinary skills with a beautiful presentation. Like the Argentine cut of beef called "matambre," the roast is butterflied open and stuffed with colorful ingredients. Then it's rolled and roasted until juicy so that when it's carved, a pinwheel of olives, spinach, ricotta cheese and red peppers is revealed. A little chimichurri on the side will make this one to remember.

4 lb (1.8 kg) center-cut boneless pork loin

8 strips bacon

¼ cup (60 mL) yellow mustard

Salt and pepper

1 (300 g) pkg frozen chopped spinach, thawed and squeezed to remove water

1 cup (250 mL) roasted red peppers

1 cup (250 mL) ricotta cheese

½ cup (125 mL) whole pimiento-stuffed green olives

1 recipe Chimichurri (page 203), for serving

1 Preheat the oven to 325°F (160°C) and place a roasting rack inside a roasting pan.

2 To butterfly the loin, think of cutting it open in a spiral fashion. Using a sharp filet or paring knife, make a ½-inch (1 cm) deep lengthwise cut down the loin, starting at the edge where the fat starts. Keep cutting at this depth/thickness as you rotate the loin, progressively working toward the center so that when it is opened, it lies flat in a rectangle (1). (You're basically tracing the pattern of the spiral with your knife.) Place the meat between a cut-open resealable plastic bag and use a meat mallet to pound the meat out to an even ½-inch (1 cm) thickness. The meat should form a rectangle about 10 x 20 inches (25 x 50 cm).

3 For the outer bacon layer, stretch the bacon slices to about 1½ times their length. Cut a piece of parchment paper that's slightly larger than the butterflied loin, and lay the bacon pieces side by side on the parchment. The bacon should line up parallel to the long side of the parchment, but only cover half of the paper. Place the loin on top of the bacon so that the grain of the meat runs perpendicular to the bacon. Brush the mustard across the surface of the meat and season with salt and pepper.

CONTINUES

ROASTS AND B G CUTS

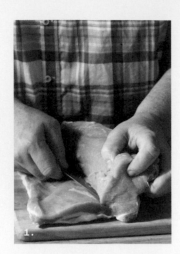  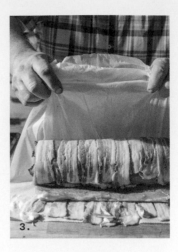

4   Starting at a short end of the meat, spread out half of the
    spinach in a 3-inch (8 cm) wide strip, following the short side.
    Repeat this with half of the roasted peppers, running alongside
    the spinach and at the same width. Spread the ricotta next to the
    peppers. Then start again with rows of the remaining spinach,
    peppers and ricotta, but leave 2 inches (5 cm) bare at the end.
    Arrange the olives in a single row at the short end where you
    started with the spinach. You are adding the fillings in blocks for
    color and texture (2).

5   Starting at the end with the olives, carefully roll up the meat into
    a spiral, using the parchment paper to help press and secure the
    fillings in place (but don't roll the parchment into the spiral!) (3).
    Halfway through, pull up the bacon with the meat, so that the
    bacon envelops the outside of the roast.

6   Lift the roast onto the rack in the roasting pan and roast, uncov-
    ered, until the roast reaches an internal temperature of 145°F
    (63°C), about 1½ hours. Remove from the pan to a cutting board to
    rest for 5 minutes before carving into ½-inch (1 cm) slices. Lay out
    the slices family-style on a platter, or place 2 on each plate to
    show off the colorful pinwheel pattern. Serve with the chimichurri.

Notes:

+   Take your time as you but-
    terfly the meat to avoid
    cutting holes in it. This is
    truly the sort of task that
    gets easier each time you

try. A decent-quality meat
mallet will help flatten
the meat to make the spiral
garnish look great from one
end to the other.

Savory Corn Pudding

Like a "tamale," this corn pudding is sweet, dense and fragrant. It soaks up the juices from the spice-braised meat, making this a real comfort food dish or, as Anna calls it, "spoon food" (referring to the enthusiasm of my eating).

1 Preheat the oven to 325°F (160°C) and butter a large 12-inch (2.5 L) oval casserole dish.

2 Whisk the masa, baking powder and salt in a large bowl to combine, and then whisk in the eggs, milk, salsa, cheese, corn and sour cream until well-combined. Pour the batter into the prepared pan, top with bread crumbs and bake until it has puffed up and is golden brown, about 1 hour.

1 Tbsp (15 mL) butter

1 cup (250 mL) masa harina or cornmeal (see note)

1 tsp (5 mL) baking powder

1 tsp (5 mL) fine salt

2 large eggs

1 cup (250 mL) 2% milk

1 cup (250 mL) prepared tomato salsa

1 cup (250 mL) grated medium cheddar cheese

1 cup (250 mL) frozen corn

½ cup (125 mL) sour cream

⅓ cup (80 mL) dry bread crumbs

221

Notes:

+ Masa harina is finely ground corn flour that has been prepared with lime. It's used for the dough to make tortillas and the filling for tamales. It's available in supermarkets (I use Maseca brand), though you could also substitute fine cornmeal in this recipe. This dish would be a great brunch item served with eggs, reheated sirloin on the side, avocado slices, queso fresco and fresh salsa. *Arriba!*

Braised Sirloin

with Peppers, Chili & Chocolate

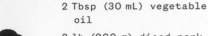

2 Tbsp (30 mL) vegetable oil

2 lb (900 g) diced pork sirloin or lean shoulder

1 medium onion, diced

2 carrots, peeled and diced

1 stalk celery, diced

2 red bell peppers, seeded and diced

1 clove garlic, crushed

¼ cup (60 mL) all-purpose flour

2 sprigs fresh thyme

1 bay leaf

2 cups (500 mL) lager beer or chicken stock

2 Tbsp (30 mL) fancy molasses

1 Tbsp (15 mL) ground coriander

1 Tbsp (15 mL) dried chili flakes

1 Tbsp (15 mL) paprika

2 oz (60 g) bittersweet chocolate, chopped

Salt and pepper

Savory Corn Pudding (page 221)

This recipe is one of the great food matches for a bold, tannic red wine. The meat is melt-away tender and loaded with a sweet vegetable background, but the full character comes through from the layering of spices and the silky finish of bittersweet chocolate that sews it all together. A ladleful of this stew with a scoop of Savory Corn Pudding (page 221) and a glass of Cabernet... oh yes, please.

1 Preheat the oven to 325°F (160°C).

2 Add the oil to a large Dutch oven over medium-high heat and sear the meat on all sides, stirring occasionally, until lightly golden, about 5 minutes. Transfer the meat to a plate, reduce the heat to medium and add the onion, carrots, celery and bell peppers to the pan. Sauté over medium heat until the onion softens slightly, about 5 minutes. Stir in the flour, thyme and bay leaf, and cook, stirring, until the flour develops a golden color, about 5 minutes. Return the meat to the pot, then add the beer, molasses, coriander, chili flakes and paprika. Stir and bring to a simmer, then cover and cook in the oven for 1 hour, until the carrots are getting soft and the meat can be crushed with a spoon.

3 Remove the pan from the oven and stir in the chocolate until it is melted and smooth (it may look grainy at first, but it will smooth out). Return to the oven until the sauce is silky and the meat is tender but still juicy, about 30 minutes more. Season to taste.

4 Ladle into pasta bowls over corn pudding or serve with warm tortillas.

Notes:

+ Chocolate that is labeled "50% cocoa" or higher will be suitable for this recipe. The higher the percentage of cocoa mass, the less sugar. Milk chocolate, for example, has only about 10% cocoa and a lot of sugar and cocoa butter. It's nice for a snack, but it doesn't have the savory, bitter flavor we look for in this recipe, which is patterned after a Mexican mole poblano sauce.

YIELD: 4-6
SERVINGS

PREP TIME:
15 MINUTES

COOK TIME:
2 ½ HOURS

Braised Country Style Ribs

"Lee Garden Style"

The exotic aroma of five-spice reminds me of my favorite Chinese restaurant in Toronto, called Lee Garden (which, sadly, closed in 2017). I used to dine there late at night on Sundays with restaurant friends, and later went with my wife and daughter after becoming a civilian. It was memorable for its excellent cooking, the always jam-packed dining room, its steamy windows that looked out to Spadina Avenue and the "hustle" service, in which they would clear the table by grabbing the plastic tablecloth and gathering the dirty dishes up like a scoop net.

1   Preheat the oven to 325°F (160°C). If the ribs are in one large piece, cut into individual rib sections by slicing through the meat between each rib bone.

2   Place the oil in an ovenproof heavy-bottomed skillet over medium-high heat, then add the onion and celery. Sauté until the onion begins to soften, 3 to 4 minutes. Stir in the jalapeño, ginger and garlic, and sauté for 1 minute more. Stir in the soy sauce, brown sugar and Chinese five spice. Stir in 2 cups (500 mL) of water and bring to a simmer.

3   Add the ribs to the sauce in a single layer and return to a simmer. Lower the heat to medium-low, cover and transfer to the oven to cook, turning the pork after the first hour, until the meat is fork-tender, about 2 hours. Use tongs to transfer the pork to a bowl to rest, and skim off excess fat from the surface of the braising liquid.

4   Place the skillet back over medium heat. Whisk the cornstarch with ¼ cup (60 mL) of cold water and pour it into the braising liquid while stirring—it will thicken as it comes to a boil. Return the ribs to the sauce to coat and keep warm.

5   Serve over cooked rice, with a side of cooked bok choy.

2 lb (900 g) country-style ribs

1 Tbsp (15 mL) vegetable oil

1 medium onion, diced

1 stalk celery, diced

1 fresh jalapeño pepper, diced

2 Tbsp (30 mL) finely grated fresh ginger

2 cloves garlic, minced

6 Tbsp (90 mL) soy sauce

3 Tbsp (45 mL) packed light brown sugar

1 tsp (5 mL) Chinese five spice powder

2 tsp (10 mL) cornstarch

8 cups (1.8 L) cooked rice, for serving

4 cups (1 L) cooked bok choy sprinkled with sesame seeds, for serving

225

Notes:

Braised meats can be cooked on the stovetop using a heavy-bottomed pot with a lid. I prefer the oven method, however, because the heat comes from all around the pot rather than from just one direction. If the pot doesn't have a lid, simply use foil.

1.

2.

3.

Oven Braised Pulled Pork

Ah, low-and-slow pulled pork. Picture a hot, lazy afternoon spent lounging in a rocking chair, nursing a cold beer with the dog sleeping at your feet, taking all day to smoke a pork shoulder until it falls apart into its sticky sweet and sour BBQ glaze. Except it's winter in Canada, and it is freezing out there! This is how I get that same tender BBQ pork sandwich glory when we are cooking indoors.

1 Preheat the oven to 325°F (160°C).

2 Combine the brown sugar, mustard, chili powder, salt, pepper and garlic powder, and rub it all over the pork (using your hands is best for this). Stir together the beer, vinegar, molasses and BBQ sauce in a Dutch oven or roasting pan, and place the seasoned pork inside. Cover and roast in the oven, basting occasionally with the juices from the pan, until the meat pulls away easily when you twist it with a fork, 3 to 4 hours (1,2).

3 Transfer the pot from the oven to a cooling rack and rest for 15 minutes (remove any butcher's string or skin). Use two forks to pull the meat apart into large shreds (3). You can cover and return the pot to the oven to reheat if necessary.

4 To serve, spoon some of the juices onto each side of a split sand-wich bun, fill it with the pulled pork and top with coleslaw. Serve with plenty of napkins and cold beer.

⅓ cup (80 mL) packed light brown sugar

2 Tbsp (30 mL) yellow mustard

2 Tbsp (30 mL) chili powder

1 Tbsp (15 mL) fine salt

1 Tbsp (15 mL) ground black pepper

1 Tbsp (15 mL) garlic powder

5 lb (2.2 kg) boneless pork shoulder

12 oz (375 mL) dark beer

1 cup (250 mL) white vinegar

½ cup (125 mL) fancy molasses

½ cup (125 mL) prepared BBQ sauce

12 sandwich buns

1 recipe Coleslaw (page 257)

Notes:

+ Using a slow cooker is another ideal means to make pulled pork indoors. Follow the manufacturer's instructions, but basically place everything in the cooker, set it for 8 hours, and you're good to go.

+ One key to making perfectly pulled pork is to avoid shredding the meat too much. Leaving bite-sized chunks provides a satisfying texture, especially for the outside "bark." You don't want this to look like tuna salad.

 YIELD: 8 SERVINGS

 PREP TIME:
30 MINUTES,
PLUS CHILLING

 COOK TIME:
2½ HOURS,
PLUS RESTING

Crispy Pork Belly

The thunderous crunch of this pork belly dish will make you a famous chef within your circle of friends. Get used to the popularity—they will invite you over to parties only for your food, not for your company ... it's a tough life! This recipe takes 2 days, but the results are well worth the effort. Crispy, salty pork in a cool lettuce wrap with lime, cucumber, cilantro, sweet hoisin and, finally, a blast of chili heat from the hot sauce: each bite is a delicious mouthful, like the flavors from your favorite Vietnamese restaurant.

2½ lb (1.1 kg) fresh pork belly

1 Tbsp (15 mL) table salt

1 tsp (5 mL) baking powder

FOR SERVING

1 head romaine lettuce, washed and separated

½ cup (125 mL) hoisin sauce

¼ cup (60 mL) sriracha sauce

2 limes, cut in wedges

1 English cucumber, washed and sliced

Fresh cilantro leaves and stems, washed

229

ROASTS AND BIG CUTS

DAY ONE:

1 Line a baking sheet with foil, place a rack overtop and set aside. Using a very sharp paring knife or box cutter, score the skin of the pork belly, cutting through the skin and just into the fat, but not through the meat. Make the cuts every ¼ inch (6 mm) across the skin side.

2 Stir together the salt and baking powder and rub it into the surface of the skin, really using your hands to massage it in. Place the pork on the prepared baking sheet and refrigerate, uncovered, overnight. (Leaving the meat exposed to the air will help dry out the skin.)

DAY TWO:

1 Preheat the oven to 325°F (160°C), and allow the pork to sit on the counter for 20 minutes to lose its chill.

2 Roast the pork on the prepared baking sheet for 1½ hours, then lower the temperature to 300°F (150°C). Continue to cook until the meat is fully cooked, the skin is light brown, there is a lot of liquid fat in the tray and the internal temperature reaches 185°F (85°C), about 45 minutes more. Remove the tray from the oven and let cool for about 30 minutes, until the pork is easy to handle. While the pork is still warm, drain off the liquid fat.

CONTINUES

3   Turn the oven up to 450°F (230°C). Place the pork back on the rack over the tray to roast until you see the skin side blistering and getting a full golden brown in color, 10 to 15 minutes. (Avoid touching the skin, as it will burn your fingers!)

4   Transfer the pork to a cutting board and rest for 5 minutes, until you can touch it without burning your fingers. Split the pork open horizontally, like a book, so that both the crisp skin and the crunchy meat sides are face down on the cutting board. This will make carving the meat easier, as you'll start slicing through the tender meat, then finish through the crispy part. Cut into ½-inch (1 cm) pieces.

5   Set out all the serving ingredients. Guests can dress their own lettuce wraps: place a piece of crispy pork on a lettuce leaf, then add the hoisin, sriracha, limes, cucumber and cilantro. You can also do this with tortillas or slider buns.

Notes:

+   The two-stage cooking method is very important—the initial low-temperature roasting cooks the meat until tender and releases the fat so that the second higher temperature makes the skin impossibly crunchy, like a potato chip. You can do the first stage of cooking up to 2 days ahead of the final—just give it extra time in the oven to crisp and reheat.

Braised Blade Roast

in Soy, Whiskey, Brown Sugar & Ginger

The dark brown shine on this roast will have you sneaking little bits before you carve it up for a Sunday dinner. It's a little sweet and a little salty, with a hint of ginger perfume in the background. It reminds me of a dish we served when I worked at Toronto's Le Sélect Bistro back in the '80s—it does not sound French at all, but the shoulder would marinate overnight, then slow-roast to a pale, juicy pink. I'd slice it and serve with just a little of the pan drippings and lots of buttered cauliflower, broccoli, carrots and creamy scalloped potatoes.

4½ lb (2 kg) boneless blade roast

1 carrot, peeled and diced

1 stalk celery, diced

1 leek, washed and diced

½ cup (125 mL) packed light brown sugar

¼ cup (60 mL) whiskey

3 Tbsp (45 mL) soy sauce

2 Tbsp (30 mL) finely grated fresh ginger

2 tsp (10 mL) dried chili flakes

1   Preheat the oven to 350°F (180°C).

2   Place the roast in a large Dutch oven with a tight-fitting lid. Place the carrot, celery, leek, brown sugar, whiskey, soy sauce, ginger and chili flakes in the Dutch oven, stir to combine and bring to a simmer over medium-high heat. Cover and transfer to the oven to cook until an inserted fork comes out easily, about 2½ hours. Uncover the roast and cook, basting often with the sauce, until the roast has a shiny coating, about 30 minutes more. The sauce will have a thick, syrupy consistency, so if it gets too thick, just add ½ cup (125 mL) water to loosen.

3   Remove the roast to a cutting board to rest for 10 minutes before removing any butcher's string and carving into thick slices. It will fall apart like a pot roast, so don't worry about getting accurate, pretty slices. Serve with a spoonful of the pan juices over steamed rice and vegetables.

Notes:

+   This is one of those roasts that you know will produce amazing meals from the leftovers: it's great sliced over a salad, diced for a quick stir-fry or just reheated for a delicious lunch kit at work.

 YIELD: 8-10
SERVINGS

 PREP TIME:
20 MINUTES

 COOK TIME:
90 MINUTES

Shoulder Carnitas

for Tacos and . . .

3 lb (1.4 kg) boneless pork shoulder roast

¼ cup (60 mL) vegetable oil

2 Tbsp (30 mL) paprika

1 Tbsp (15 mL) fine salt

2 tsp (10 mL) ground cumin

2 tsp (10 mL) ground coriander

1 tsp (5 mL) ground cinnamon

1 tsp (5 mL) dried oregano

1 medium onion, diced

1 stalk celery, diced

1 red bell pepper, seeded and diced

2 jalapeño peppers, seeded and sliced

1 orange, cut in 6 wedges

1 lime, cut in 6 wedges

2 cloves garlic, crushed

Tortillas, cooked rice and your favorite taco toppings (such as shredded cabbage, guacamole, salsa, sour cream, lime wedges, toasted pumpkin seeds, pomegranate seeds, cilantro and lots of hot sauce), for serving

There are great taco fillings that take very little time (see Mexican Chorizo Taco Mix, page 128), but there are others that are worth the wait. This slow-braised shoulder fills the kitchen with amazing aromas that remind me of a complicated preparation called "al Pibil," which is pork shoulder baked in banana leaves with spices and lime. When I made Tacos al Pibil, there were a number of ingredients that were not easy to find, so I've come up with this version instead, which I think is just as fulfilling. The aroma of spices, citrus and chilies makes it taste like a loving *abuelita* made it for you.

---

1 Preheat the oven to 350°F (180°C). Cut the shoulder roast into large chunks, about 3 inches (8 cm) square. Toss the meat with the oil, paprika, salt, cumin, coriander, cinnamon and oregano in a large bowl.

2 Place the onion, celery, bell pepper, jalapeños, orange, lime and garlic in a large Dutch oven with a lid. Arrange the spice-covered meat on top of the vegetables in a single layer. Cover the pan and heat it on the stovetop over medium-high until you can hear the onion sizzling, about 3 minutes.

3 Transfer the covered pan to the oven, roast for 1 hour, then remove the lid and roast until the meat crushes easily with a spoon, about 30 minutes more. Remove the pan from the oven to cool on a rack for 5 minutes, and skim off any fat from the surface.

4 Shred the meat using two forks (like for Oven Braised Pulled Pork, page 227), then stir the meat back into the pan juices and serve with the tortillas, rice and toppings.

Notes:

+ The carnitas can be left as chunks instead of "pulling"—when decorated with the colorful toppings, this makes an attractive dish on a taco buffet.

Kielbasa Stuffed Pork Rack

with Honey Mustard Glaze

This is an impressive-looking stuffed roast, because the center of each slice has a perfectly round filling. The kielbasa is full of smoky garlic flavor that seasons the fresh rack and absolutely drinks up the honey mustard glaze. I get my pork rack from my local butcher, Niagara Sausage, and they also make their own kielbasa, so it's a one-stop pork shop.

1 Preheat the oven to 350°F (180°C).

2 To butterfly the pork, make a cut into the pork loin that follows the line of the bones down the length of the pork but turns to follow the bottom of the eye. The thickness of the meat once opened will be about ¾ inch (2 cm). Keep cutting this thickness in a spiral, so that the rack essentially unrolls like a carpet—it will be about 8 inches (20 cm) square with the rib bones attached to one side.

3 Peel the outer skin from the kielbasa (1) and trim it to the width of the pork rack (cut any excess into ½-inch (1 cm) coins to put in the roasting pan). Place the kielbasa along the side of the pork opposite to the bones and roll the pork up, enveloping the kielbasa, until you reach the bones. Tie the roast in between each bone with butcher's twine (2). Arrange the sliced onion in the bottom of a roasting pan, place the tied roast on top and season lightly. Arrange any extra kielbasa slices in the pan.

ROAST

2¼ lb (1 kg) center-cut pork rack (4 bones)

10 oz (280 g) kielbasa sausage (as straight of a piece as possible)

½ medium onion, sliced

Salt and pepper

GLAZE

½ cup (125 mL) honey

½ cup (125 mL) grainy mustard

¼ cup (60 mL) dry white wine

2 tsp (10 mL) chopped fresh thyme, leaves only

Salt and pepper

CONTINUES

4   Prepare the glaze by whisking together the honey, mustard, wine and thyme. Roast the pork until the pork (not the kielbasa—it is already fully cooked) reaches an internal temperature of 145°F (63°C), about 1½ hours. After the first 20 minutes of roasting, brush the top and sides of the roast with the glaze and repeat this every 10 to 15 minutes. (The roast will take all of the glaze, but by the time the roast is done, the liquid glaze, juices from the roast and the onion and kielbasa slices make a complete sauce.) (3, previous page)

5   Remove the roast from the pan to a cutting board to rest for 5 minutes. Remove the butcher's twine and carve thick slices so that each portion has a bone. Serve the pork with the sauce from the pan.

Notes:

+   If the kielbasa has a curve to it, make a series of ½-inch (1.2 cm) cuts into the inside of the bend and gently pull to straighten it. Most coiled kielbasa has a tough, inedible paper-like casing that is meant to be removed. Be sure to remove the outer skin from the kielbasa! Kielbasa comes in several forms, including lean and double-smoked, but I prefer the regular one, as it stays moist during cooking and tends to be just the right diameter to fit inside the rack.

YIELD:
MAKES 5 CUPS
(1.25 L)

PREP TIME:
20 MINUTES

COOK TIME:
15 MINUTES

Welland Market Relish

Our local farmer's market operates year-round, but the high season is from June to October, with the offerings changing weekly. This recipe is a ray of sunshine for colder days when you're thirsting for some of the summer's warmth. It will keep in the fridge for 2 weeks, covered, but will be gone long before that.

1 Place the eggplant, zucchini, onion, celery, cucumber, bell pepper and jalapeño peppers in a saucepot with a lid. Cover with the vinegar and bring to a boil over medium-high heat. Reduce the heat to medium and simmer, covered, until the vegetables are tender, about 10 minutes.

2 Add the brown sugar, celery salt and pie spice, stirring to mix.

3 Add the tomatoes and peaches, then return the relish to a simmer and cook, uncovered, for 5 to 8 minutes, to make sure that they are cooked to the same texture as the other ingredients.

4 Let cool completely before transferring to an airtight container. The relish will keep in the fridge for up to 2 weeks.

1 cup (250 mL) diced peeled eggplant

1 cup (250 mL) diced zucchini (ends trimmed)

½ cup (125 mL) diced yellow onion

½ cup (125 mL) diced celery

½ cup (125 mL) diced cucumber

½ cup (125 mL) seeded and diced red bell pepper

3 jalapeño peppers, seeded and thinly sliced

1 cup (250 mL) white vinegar

½ cup (125 mL) packed brown sugar

1 tsp (5 mL) celery salt

1 tsp (5 mL) pumpkin pie spice

1 cup (250 mL) diced fresh tomatoes

1 cup (250 mL) diced pitted peeled peaches

239

ROASTS AND BIG CUTS

CONTINUES

Notes:

+ You will be able to find the ingredients for this recipe in your local stores, even off-season. You can adjust to your taste with more or fewer jalapeños, or switch out the peaches for a different fruit, like apples or pears. It's a versatile accompaniment, wonderful with hot dishes, or sandwiches or cold cuts.

Boneless Loin in Black Pepper Mustard

with Welland Market Relish

240

3 Tbsp (45 mL) Dijon
  mustard

2 tsp (10 mL) ground black
  pepper

2 tsp (10 mL) fine salt

1 tsp (5 mL) chopped fresh
  thyme, leaves only

2 lb (900 g) boneless
  pork loin roast

This is quite a simple roast dinner but will become a go-to recipe for entertaining, as it is so delicious and easy to accomplish. A few slices of tender, juicy pork with a homemade tangy, heat-kissed relish will have you thinking about making a sandwich for tomorrow's lunch with the leftovers (if there are any). The key is to monitor the temperature and not overcook this roast.

———

1 Preheat the oven to 350°F (180°C) and place a rack in a roasting pan. Stir together the mustard, pepper, salt and thyme, then rub it all over the pork loin roast (using your hands is easiest). Place the roast on the rack in the pan and cook, uncovered, until it reaches an internal temperature of 145°F (63°C), 50 to 60 minutes. Remove the roast to rest on a cutting board for 5 minutes.

2 Once the roast has rested, carve it into thin slices and serve with some of the relish on top and the remainder in a side dish.

Notes:

+ This is where I rely on a digital thermometer inserted into the center of the roast to alert me to when the meat gets to the right internal temperature. Say goodbye to dry, over-cooked roast!

Ukrainian Treasure Chest

Tenderloin Stuffed with Perogies, Onion & Bacon

Who knew that these little pillows of potato and cheese could be used to stuff a pork roast? My wife, Anna, suggested I try perogies as a stuffing for a roast tenderloin, and when I cut the first slice, I exclaimed, "It's like a Ukrainian treasure chest!" This dish is a bit of a magic trick, as it yields such a welcome surprise when you slice into it—recognizable and delicious, the perogies are deeply satisfying. To serve it, you only need a big dollop of sour cream as a sauce.

2 pork tenderloins
   (2 lb/900 g total)

3 strips bacon, diced

½ cup (125 mL) diced onion

1½ lb (675 g) perogies

Salt and pepper

1 cup (250 mL) sour cream

2 green onions, thinly
   sliced

1 Sauté the bacon and onion together in a sauté pan over medium heat, until the onion is soft, 8 to 10 minutes. The bacon will not be crisp. Set aside to cool.

2 Cook the perogies in a large pot of boiling salted water until they float (follow the package instructions for timing). Drain them in a colander, transfer to a dish and toss with the cooked bacon and onion, then let cool to room temperature (1, next page).

3 Pat the tenderloins dry with a paper towel. Use a knife with a thin blade to remove the silver skin (see page 21 for tips) and then make a cut lengthwise into the thickest part of the head to butterfly the tenderloin. The cut should go nearly but not all the way through in order to open up the surface area. Using short knife strokes, make a series of 4 to 6 cuts from head to tail through the thick parts to open like a book. Lay the butterflied tenderloin inside a cut-open resealable plastic bag and hammer gently with a meat tenderizer until even in thickness, about ¼ inch (6 mm).

4 Preheat the oven to 350°F (180°C) and place a rack inside a roasting pan.

CONTINUES

1.

2.

3.

5   Lay one of the flattened tenderloins on a cutting board and spoon the cooled perogy mixture on top, covering the meat but not quite going to the edges (2). Place the second tenderloin on top in the opposite way, so that the wide end of the bottom tenderloin meets the narrow end of the top one. Form into a cylinder (the cooled perogies will help hold the cylindrical shape) and tie the roast with 4 to 6 pieces of butcher's twine to keep its shape (3).

6   Season the roast with salt and pepper and place on the rack set in the roasting pan. Cook, uncovered, until the middle of the stuffing reaches 155°F (68°C), 35 to 40 minutes. Transfer to a cutting board to rest. Remove the butcher's twine and slice the tenderloin roast into thick slices. Serve with the sour cream and green onions.

Crisp Roast Belly & Tenderloin Porchetta

with Fennel Slaw

I've seen this Italian roast pork in many forms—as a whole animal, full loin, boneless shoulder or belly alone—but it's always a special treat. Making my porchetta is a big production, but it is perfect for a hungry crowd, and the "oohs and ahs" you'll get when your guests see the crisp crackling and slices of belly-wrapped tenderloin will make you blush. The roast is carved into slices to stuff into rolls with a fresh fennel slaw, but you should also keep a jar of hot pepper sauce nearby in case I show up.

---

1   Do this first step a day ahead. Using a sharp paring knife or box cutter, score the skin of the pork belly in a diamond pattern (cutting every ½ inch/1 cm), just through the skin and not into the meat. Mix together 1 Tbsp (15 mL) of the salt and the baking powder, and season the skin with the mixture. Chill overnight, uncovered, to dry out the skin and make it crispy.

2   The next day, preheat the oven to 300°F (150°C) and set a roasting rack over a tray or baking dish. (Fat will collect in the pan, so made sure it is deep enough and easy to handle.)

3   Pat the skin side of the pork belly dry with a paper towel and lay it, skin side down, on a cutting board. Using a sharp knife, score the meat side every ¾ inch (2 cm) to a depth of ½ inch (1 cm) to allow the seasoning to get into the meat (1).

6½ lb (3 kg) fresh pork belly, skin on

2 Tbsp (30 mL) table salt, divided

1 tsp (5 mL) baking powder

1 medium onion, diced

1 navel orange, peeled, cut in quarters, seeds removed

2 cloves garlic

1 Tbsp (15 mL) ground black pepper

2 pork tenderloins (2 lb/900 g total)

FENNEL SLAW

1 bulb fennel, trimmed and thinly sliced

1 small red onion, thinly sliced

½ head green cabbage, trimmed and thinly sliced

1 Tbsp (15 mL) olive oil

24 panini (crusty rolls)

CONTINUES

Notes:

+ A tip for tying the roast is to cut 6 or 8 lengths of butcher's twine and place them under the belly at intervals before filling it—then they will be in place to tie after the porchetta is assembled and rolled.

+ Whenever you drain clear fat from large cuts like belly roast, you can use it for roasting potatoes, searing chops or making candles (page 278).

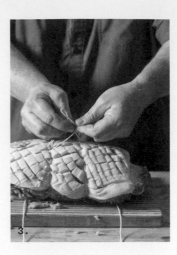

4   Pulse the onion, orange, garlic, remaining 1 Tbsp (15 mL) salt and pepper in a food processor to a smooth paste. Reserve 2 Tbsp (30 mL) of this mixture for the coleslaw. Spread the remainder of the mixture over the meat side of the belly (2).

5   Remove any silver skin from the two tenderloins (see page 21 for tips), and place them across the belly, head to tail (so there is an even layer of tenderloin), then roll up the belly around the paste and tenderloins, and tie firmly with butcher's twine (3). Place the belly roast, seam side down, on the roasting rack set on the prepared baking sheet. Roast until the skin is starting to get crispy and light brown, the tenderloin reaches an internal temperature of 140°F (60°C) and the surrounding belly is 165°F (74°C), about 3½ hours.

6   Remove the roast and increase the oven to 425°F (218°C). Carefully drain off the rendered fat and reserve for later use. Return the roast to the oven until the skin is puffed and deep golden brown in color, about 30 minutes. Remove from the oven and rest for 10 minutes before slicing.

7   To make the slaw, toss the fennel, onion, cabbage, oil and reserved 2 Tbsp (30 mL) of orange paste together until evenly combined. (This can be done while the pork is roasting and kept in the fridge.)

8   To serve, untie the roast, remove the crispy skin and cut it into ½-inch (1 cm) pieces so that a few bits can be added to each portion. Slice the meat into thin slices and place a few into a panini with some of the crispy skin and fennel slaw.

Milk Braised Capicola

with Root Vegetables & Horseradish

3 cups (750 mL) 2% milk

1 leek, washed and diced

2 large parsnips, peeled and diced

2 large carrots, peeled and diced

2 sprigs fresh thyme

1 bay leaf

1½ tsp (7 mL) coarse salt

3½ lb (1.6 kg) fresh capicola (shoulder) roast

Chopped fresh Italian parsley, for garnish

2 Tbsp (30 mL) prepared horseradish, for serving

When I was a kid, we'd have a "boiled dinner," where the chunks of meat were served with a broth and plenty of vegetables. I would doctor my own portion by mashing the vegetables into the soup and adding lots of black pepper. This recipe braises the meat to an impossibly tender state, and then the vegetables are pureed into the liquid to make a luxurious sauce, spiked with the heat of horseradish.

---

1 Preheat the oven to 300°F (150°C).

2 Bring the milk, leek, parsnips, carrots, thyme, bay leaf and salt to a simmer in a large Dutch oven over medium-high heat. Place the roast in the center of the pan, cover, and cook in the oven until fork-tender, about 3½ hours. (The milk will have separated but don't worry about it.)

3 Remove the roast to a cutting board to keep warm. Discard the thyme sprigs and bay leaf. Using an immersion blender, puree the vegetables into the pan juices to create a sauce (or transfer to a blender to puree). Season to taste.

4 Cut the roast into thick slices, spoon lots of the sauce overtop and sprinkle with parsley. Serve horseradish on the side. This is nice with a side of egg noodles or buttered boiled potatoes.

Notes:

+ This meat is fall-apart tender like a pot roast, so it will stay juicy and can be reheated in the sauce as leftovers. It's not dark brown like most pot roasts, and it has a more delicate flavor from all the vegetables and milk, so the horseradish works well as a condiment to bring out the sweet flavors of the root vegetables.

Roast Picnic Shoulder

with Apple Onion Gravy

A weekend dinner that takes a bit of time, fills the house with wonderful aromas and puts a grin on your family's faces is the sort of thing that gives me great satisfaction. This classic combination of juicy roast pork with a brown sauce loaded with the natural sweetness of onions and apples is a memory maker. And don't worry, there will be plenty of gravy.

1 Tbsp (15 mL) fine salt, plus extra for seasoning

1 tsp (5 mL) baking powder

3 lb (1.4 kg) picnic shoulder roast, skin on

2 Granny Smith apples, peeled and diced

1 medium onion, diced

⅓ cup (80 mL) all-purpose flour

4 cups (1 L) chicken stock, divided

Ground black pepper

251

RCASTS AND BIG CUTS

1 Preheat the oven to 350°F (180°C) and combine 1 Tbsp (15 mL) of the salt with the baking powder. Using a box cutter, score the skin of the pork and season all over with the salt mixture. Place the pork in a roasting pan and roast, uncovered, basting occasionally with the pan drippings, for 1½ hours. After the first 45 minutes, add half of the apples and all of the onion, and toss to coat in the drippings.

2 Increase the oven to 450°F (230°C) and roast the pork, basting occasionally, until the skin crisps up, about 35 minutes more.

3 Remove the roasting pan from the oven, and place the pork on a plate or cutting board to rest while the sauce is prepared. Using a slotted spoon, remove the onion and apples from the pan and reserve. Drain and discard all but ¼ cup (60 mL) of the drippings from the pan. Stir the flour into the drippings and cook over medium heat until it turns a nutty brown color, about 10 minutes. Slowly pour in 1 cup (250 mL) of the stock while whisking constantly, and let it thicken before slowly adding the remaining 3 cups (750 mL) of

CONTINUES

Notes:

+ You can use this same method with a boneless picnic roast, but either way, I always look for ones that have the skin on for the texture of the crisp crackling. After carving, remove any bits of meat left on the bone and add to the gravy with leftover slices for a beautiful hot roast pork sandwich.

stock. Stir the reserved cooked apples and onion back into the pan (they will basically dissolve into the sauce) and add the remaining uncooked apples. Simmer for about 5 minutes to cook the apples, and season to taste.

4   To serve, using a serrated knife, cut the pork through the crisp skin toward the bone into ½-inch (1 cm) slices. Place 1 or 2 slices on each plate and spoon some of the gravy overtop. Serve the remaining gravy in a sauceboat.

Anna's "Cottage Boil" Vegetables

Summer cookouts are all about keeping things simple. I'll buy fresh produce at the farmers' market and light the grill for the meat, maybe slice a tomato or two and look forward to this excellent side dish. A single pot of water is used to cook the vegetables in order according to their necessary cooking time, and they are simply dressed with a little butter, herbs, salt and pepper.

1 lb (450 g) new mini potatoes, scrubbed

Salt

8 carrots, peeled and halved but tops left on

4 cobs corn, shucked and broken in half

½ lb (225 g) green or yellow beans, ends trimmed

2 Tbsp (30 mL) butter

2 Tbsp (30 mL) chopped fresh Italian parsley or chives

Ground black pepper

ROASTS AND BIG CUTS

---

1   Put the potatoes in a large pot and cover with 16 cups (4 L) of cold water and enough salt to taste it. Bring to a boil over high heat, uncovered, and then reduce the heat to medium-high and simmer for 5 minutes (the potatoes will only be partially cooked at this point). Add the carrots and cook for 3 minutes more, then add the corn and cook for 2 minutes more. Finally, drop in the beans and cook until they squeak when you bite one, about 3 minutes.

2   Drain the vegetables and dress with the butter and parsley, and season to taste. Serve in a giant bowl with a pair of tongs.

Notes:

+   Anna and I love cooking together. Often it's me on the grill, and Anna does the sides (but not always). This dish is referred to as the "Cottage Boil" not only because that's the place we make it most often, but also because we just don't want to have to wash more than one pot!

Low-and-Slow Smoky Golden Capicola Roast

LIVING HIGH OFF THE HOG

¾ cup (175 mL) yellow mustard, divided

3-4 lb (1.4-1.8 kg) fresh capicola roast

⅓ cup (80 mL) Basic BBQ Rub (page 267)

⅓ cup (80 mL) packed light brown sugar

¼ cup (60 mL) white vinegar

There are a few things that make this recipe different from pulled pork. First, the capicola is about half the size of a butt, so there is less meat to deal with (unless you're feeding a crowd, pulled pork has lots of leftovers). Second, it is cooked to a tender state but still best cut into slices like a roast, not pulled into shreds. Third, the roast is glazed with a deceptively simple but tasty golden mustard BBQ sauce rather than the more familiar red one.

1   Brush ¼ cup (60 mL) of the yellow mustard over the entire surface of the pork and then press the BBQ rub onto the mustard so the pork is fully coated.

2   If using a smoker BBQ, set it to 210°F (100°C) and cook the pork, covered, until the internal temperature reaches 185°F (85°C), 4 to 5 hours. If using a gas BBQ, place the pork in a roasting pan (not the good one) and use indirect heat (by turning on a single burner opposite the side of the grill where the meat is), maintaining the temperature over the 4 to 5 hours of cooking time.

3   While the pork is cooking, stir the remaining ½ cup (125 mL) of the mustard with the brown sugar and white vinegar, and baste the roast during the last hour of cooking to develop a golden glaze over the surface. Keep any leftover sauce to serve with the pork.

4   Remove the pork to a cutting board and rest for 5 minutes before cutting into ¼-inch (6 mm) slices. Serve with Anna's "Cottage Boil" Vegetables (page 253).

Notes:

+ Don't confuse the fresh capicola cut with the deli meat of the same name. The cold cut gets its common name from this muscle (blade capicola roast), which is actually a continuation of the loin muscle into the shoulder area. This is my favorite cut for the BBQ. It's good cooked whole or as chops (and great as Char Siu Pork Capicola, page 264). If your butcher makes sausage, they will have shoulders in the back and can prepare this cut, as it is part of the shoulder.

BBQ Pulled Pork

When I talk to fellow BBQ fans, at some point, the conversation leads to either ribs or pulled pork. When I got into cooking with charcoal and, later, pellet grills, many Saturdays were highlighted by a full day on the deck of our home, enrobed in a cloud of dizzying deliciousness from the smoke and the aroma of the pork shoulder. Yes, it takes a long time, but once you get it rolling, there is not a whole lot to do. The low-and-slow cooking caramelizes the sugar in your BBQ rub onto the surface of the meat and, of course, there's the smoky scent... well, let's just say you shouldn't be surprised if the neighbors are suddenly friendly and stopping by to borrow a cup of sugar.

1   Brush one side of the pork with half of the mustard and cover it in half of the rub. Turn it over, and do the same to the other side so that the entire surface is covered in the rub.

2   If using a smoker BBQ, set it to 210°F (100°C) and cook the pork, lid down, until the internal temperature reaches 185°F (85°C), 8 to 9 hours. If using a gas BBQ, place the pork in a roasting pan (not the good one) and use indirect heat (by turning on a single burner opposite the side of the grill where the meat is) and maintain the temperature over the 8 to 9 hours of cooking time.

3   While the pork is cooking, stir together the BBQ sauce and vinegar, and use up to half of it to baste the pork over the last hour of cooking.

CONTINUES

8-10 lb (3.6-4.5 kg) skinless boneless pork butt

½ cup (125 mL) yellow mustard

½ cup (125 mL) Basic BBQ Rub (page 267)

1 cup (250 mL) Lipstick on a Pig BBQ Sauce (page 270)

½ cup (125 mL) white vinegar

COLESLAW

½ head fresh green cabbage

1 carrot, peeled

½ cup (125 mL) mayonnaise

Juice of 1 lemon

2 tsp (10 mL) celery salt

24 dinner rolls

Notes:

+   The outside of the shoulder will caramelize and take on the smoke—this is known as the "bark." Try to break this up and work the smoke into the remainder of the meat for the best flavor. Pellet or ceramic charcoal cookers are what I prefer for this kind of BBQ. You can do it on a gas grill, but keep an eye on the temperature so it doesn't scorch. This dish keeps really well, so for a crowd, you can make it long before your guests arrive and then reheat it in the BBQ sauce.

4   Remove the pork from the smoker and let it rest on a cutting board for 30 minutes, then use two forks to pull the pork into large shreds and pieces (there is no need to break it down to a fine shred; you want to retain some texture once it is mixed into the sauce). Toss the pork with the remaining BBQ sauce and keep warm, covered, in a roasting pan on the grill at 165°F (74°C) until ready to serve.

5   For the coleslaw, grate the cabbage and carrot on the coarse side of a box grater and dress with the mayonnaise, lemon juice and celery salt. Chill until ready to serve.

6   To serve, split the dinner rolls and let your guests dress their sandwiches with the pulled pork and coleslaw.

LIVING HIGH OFF THE HOG

YIELD: 4 SERVINGS

PREP TIME:
20 MINUTES,
PLUS MARINATING

COOK TIME:
45 MINUTES

Country Ribs

in Raspberry Jalapeño BBQ Glaze

Cut from a bone-in rib roast, these are closer in texture (and in cooking time) to pork chops than ribs. Country-style ribs are tender and flavor-packed but take a fraction of the time of back or side ribs. The hot grill will kiss them with a smoky char, but the sweet and hot BBQ glaze will round out the flavor. You should already be thinking about potato salad, zucchini, sliced tomatoes and beer or wine.

1 Lay the country-style ribs across a cutting board and split in half through the lean part of the meat. Cut in between each bone section so you have individual rib portions, each with a good amount of lean meat on it (you should get between 10 and 12).

2 In a large flat dish, stir together the onion, apple cider, vinegar, jalapeño pickle juice, salt, brown sugar, coriander and cloves until the salt and sugar have dissolved. Add the ribs and turn them over at least once to ensure they are covered in the marinade. Cover and chill for at least 1 hour, and up to 24 hours. (The longer you marinate them, the more flavor the ribs will absorb.)

3 Remove the ribs from the marinade and pat them dry with a paper towel to remove any excess juice. Toss the ribs with the rub until they are fully coated.

4 Strain the marinade, measure ¾ cup (175 mL) into a small saucepot and bring to a boil over high heat. Stir in the BBQ sauce, raspberry jam and chopped jalapeños. Reduce the heat to medium and bring to a simmer, stirring, until the jam dissolves. Remove the sauce from the heat.

3 lb (1.4 kg) country-style ribs

1 medium onion, sliced

½ cup (125 mL) unsweetened apple cider

½ cup (125 mL) raspberry-flavored red wine vinegar

¼ cup (60 mL) jalapeño pickle juice (from the jar)

2 Tbsp (30 mL) coarse salt

2 Tbsp (30 mL) packed light brown sugar

1 tsp (5 mL) ground coriander

6 whole cloves or ¼ tsp (1 mL) ground

½ cup (125 mL) Basic BBQ Rub (page 267)

½ cup (125 mL) BBQ Sauce (store-bought or homemade)

¼ cup (60 mL) raspberry jam

¼ cup (60 mL) chopped pickled jalapeños

Sliced green onions, for garnish

CONTINUES

5 Preheat the grill to medium-high. Cook the ribs, with the lid closed, until they reach an internal temperature of 140°F (60°C), 10 to 12 minutes. Brush both sides of the ribs with the BBQ glaze and cook until they reach an internal temperature of 145°F (63°C), 4 to 5 minutes more. Remove to a platter to serve with the remaining BBQ glaze and green onions for garnish.

Notes:

+ Country-style ribs are not at every meat counter, so you may have to ask your butcher. The marinade acts as a brine to season the meat and keep it moist as it cooks, and the finishing glaze does a great balancing act between the sweet raspberry and hot jalapeños.

Dirty Lawyer Ribs

Quick-Cook BBQ

I was inspired to create this dish by our friend's excitement over the purchase of an electric countertop pressure cooker (he's a lawyer but is really into food). My pals in the BBQ world would be horrified at the notion of "boiling" ribs, but this really gives you a delicious result in less than 2 hours when you don't have all day to do the low-and-slow method. I also chalked up the success of this recipe to the fact that our lawyer pal charges too much per hour to justify waiting 5 hours for ribs!

2 racks back ribs (about 4½ lb/2 kg), membrane removed (see note for tips)

1 cup (250 mL) lager beer

1 clove garlic, minced

½ cup (125 mL) Lipstick on a Pig BBQ Sauce (page 270)

¼ cup (60 mL) Basic BBQ Rub (page 267)

1   Cut the ribs in half, and place them, standing up, on the rack insert set inside the pressure cooker. Add the beer and garlic, then set the cooker to high pressure for 15 minutes, according to the manufacturer's instructions.

2   Preheat the grill to 300°F (150°C).

3   Transfer the leftover cooking juices from the pressure cooker to a small saucepot over medium heat and reduce them to ¾ cup (175 mL). Stir in the BBQ sauce. Remove the pan from the heat.

4   Coat the ribs with the rub (the moisture from pressure cooking will help the rub adhere to the ribs) and cook on the grill with the lid on, basting with the BBQ sauce mixture and turning once or twice, until the rack "gives" when twisted into a C-shape with tongs, about 20 minutes.

Notes:

+   To remove the membrane from a rack of ribs, use a fork to separate the membrane from the bones slightly, then pull the membrane off with your hands.

YIELD: 8 SERVINGS

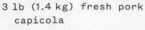

PREP TIME:
20 MINUTES,
PLUS MARINATING

COOK TIME:
30 MINUTES

Char Siu Pork Capicola

3 lb (1.4 kg) fresh pork capicola

½ cup (125 mL) ketchup

⅓ cup (80 mL) soy sauce

⅓ cup (80 mL) rice wine vinegar or white wine vinegar

⅓ cup (80 mL) honey

⅓ cup (80 mL) hoisin sauce

1 tsp (5 mL) Chinese five-spice powder

1 Tbsp (15 mL) packed light brown sugar

1 Tbsp (15 mL) sesame oil

1 tsp (5 mL) finely grated fresh ginger

8-10 dashes Worcestershire sauce

1 clove garlic, minced

Chopped roasted peanuts and fresh cilantro leaves, for sprinkling

The cooking school I attended was located in Toronto's Kensington Market, next to bustling Chinatown, so I spent a lot of time sifting through shops and grabbing a bite at one of the many noodle joints that always had window displays filled with glowing red-meat delights, especially lengths of this type of BBQ pork. Char siu is marinated in a sweet, spicy, pungent brew and then cooked at high heat to develop color, flavor and those wickedly tasty burnt ends. It can be sliced and eaten as a meal or used as an ingredient in fried rice, vegetable or noodle dishes, or in steamed bao buns as a snack.

1 Cut the pork lengthwise into ¾-inch (2 cm) slices.

2 Stir together the ketchup, soy sauce, vinegar, honey, hoisin, five-spice powder, brown sugar, sesame oil, ginger, Worcestershire and garlic in a large dish or resealable plastic bag and add the pork to marinate for up to 4 hours.

3 Heat the grill to medium-high. Remove the pork from the marinade, scraping off the excess into a bowl.

4 Grill the pork for 10 minutes per side, then baste with the marinade until the marinade is all used up and the internal temperature of the pork is 150°F (65°C), at least 5 minutes per side.

5 Remove the pork to a cutting board and let rest for 5 minutes, then cut into ¼-inch (6 mm) slices. Sprinkle with the peanuts and cilantro leaves.

Notes:

+ When I lived in Toronto, I had easy access to so many more foods like this, so when I get a craving for something like char siu, it makes sense to know how to do a reasonable version of it at home. And I make a big enough quantity to have leftovers. If you can't find a whole capicola (blade) roast, use butt end or capicola chops. Try this same marinade on other cuts, like whole tenderloin or country-style ribs.

Classic BBQ Back Ribs

Yes, you can do these ribs in your oven or on a gas grill, but I love the aroma of the smoke that comes off a pellet or charcoal grill. Be a pal and supply plenty of paper napkins, a finger bowl, a bone bowl and toothpicks for after dinner!

---

1   For the BBQ rub, stir all of the ingredients together in a large mixing bowl until evenly combined. You'll wind up with about 1½ cups (375 mL), but if you'd like to keep the rub on hand, you can easily double or triple the recipe. Store the rub in an airtight container in the pantry until ready to use. It will keep for 3 months.

2   For the mop, stir together the BBQ sauce, vinegar and beer, and chill until ready to use.

3   Brush a thin layer of mustard over both sides of the ribs (this will help the rub stick to the meat). Completely cover both sides of the ribs with the BBQ rub.

4   If using a smoker BBQ, set it to 225°F (110°C) and cook the ribs, covered, until the ribs "give" when twisted with tongs, about 3 hours. If using a gas grill, cook at the same temperature for about 3 hours using the indirect method (see page 13, "Gas Grill"). For the last hour of cooking, baste the ribs on both sides with the mop every 15 minutes. You can shut off the barbecue and rest the ribs in there, with the lid on, until ready to serve. To serve, carve between each bone to present individual ribs.

BASIC BBQ RUB

½ cup (125 mL) sweet paprika

¼ cup (60 mL) packed light brown sugar

2 Tbsp (30 mL) ground cumin

2 Tbsp (30 mL) ground coriander

2 Tbsp (30 mL) dry mustard powder

2 Tbsp (30 mL) table salt

1 Tbsp (15 mL) granulated garlic

1 Tbsp (15 mL) ground black pepper

BASIC BBQ MOP

1 cup (250 mL) BBQ sauce (store-bought or homemade)

½ cup (125 mL) apple cider vinegar

½ cup (125 mL) lager-style beer or your favorite style

3 Tbsp yellow mustard

2¼ lb (1 kg) pork back ribs, membrane removed (see note on page 263)

Notes:

+   When I do a big outdoor cookout for a gang, I get all the side dishes done while the ribs are smoking, and then when the ribs are cooked, I turn up the temperature and quickly grill sausages and chops. This way, there's a variety of barbecued meats for the meal, and everything is done at the same time.

Lipstick on a Pig BBQ Side Ribs

You'll be smiling, and there will be BBQ sauce on your face—get used to it. These classic ribs use the St. Louis (square) cut (see page 7) and will be tender but not falling off the bone. The spice rub will infuse right through the meat, and the outside will have a sticky glaze of sauce. If you prefer, skip the basting step and serve the sauce on the side.

And speaking of sauce, I'm really not trying to shut down the commercial BBQ sauce industry, but you may find yourself making your own from now on and adding a secret ingredient (bourbon, ice wine or cayenne, perhaps?) to customize it and make it yours.

2 racks (each 2¼ lb/1 kg) St. Louis cut side ribs, membrane removed (see note on page 263 for tips) (1)

⅓ cup (80 mL) yellow mustard

½ cup (125 mL) Basic BBQ Rub (page 267)

½ cup (125 mL) Lipstick on a Pig BBQ Sauce (recipe follows)

1   Brush both sides of the ribs with the yellow mustard and cover the entire surface of the ribs with the BBQ rub, pressing on the meat to help it adhere (2). The mustard helps the rib stick to the ribs.

2   If using a smoker BBQ, set it to 210°F (100°C) and cook the pork, covered, until the ribs "give" when twisted with tongs, 3 to 4 hours. If using a gas grill, cook at the same temperature for about 3 hours using the indirect method (see page 13, "Gas Grill"). For the last 45 minutes of cooking, baste the ribs regularly with the BBQ sauce. To serve, carve between each bone to present individual ribs.

1.

2.

YIELD: MAKES
ABOUT 5 CUPS
(1.25 L)

PREP TIME:
3 MINUTES

COOK TIME:
15 MINUTES

Lipstick on a Pig BBQ Sauce

1 can (28 oz/796 mL)
   crushed tomatoes

1 cup (250 mL) Basic BBQ
   Rub (page 267)

½ cup (125 mL) fancy
   molasses

½ cup (125 mL) white
   vinegar

1 Stir together the tomatoes, BBQ rub, molasses and vinegar in a medium saucepot over medium-high heat. Once the mixture reaches a full simmer, reduce the heat to medium and simmer for 10 minutes, stirring occasionally, to bring out the flavors. Use right away or let cool and refrigerate. This sauce can be kept covered in the fridge for 2 weeks.

Honey Garlic Oven Roasted Back Ribs

with Sesame Crunch

It *is* possible to cook great ribs in the oven, and this is a recipe I would use in the winter, on those days when I just don't want to cook outside. These tender ribs are brushed with honey-garlic-orange glaze and crusted with crispy bread crumbs that are so tasty you'll be licking your lips and wishing for more.

2 racks (each 2¼ lb/1 kg) back ribs, membrane removed (see note on page 263 for tips)

½ cup (125 mL) yellow mustard

½ cup (125 mL) Basic BBQ Rub (page 267)

¼ cup (60 mL) honey

2 cloves garlic, minced

Finely grated zest and juice of 2 navel oranges

⅔ cup (160 mL) dry bread crumbs

1 clove garlic, minced

2 Tbsp (30 mL) sesame seeds

1 Tbsp (15 mL) olive oil

Hot sauce (I like Frank's)

1   Preheat the oven to 350°F (180°C). Line a baking sheet with foil or parchment paper, then grease a roasting rack and place it on top of the tray.

2   Brush both sides of the ribs with an even layer of mustard and sprinkle the BBQ rub onto the ribs to cover the mustard completely. Place the ribs, bone side down, on the prepared baking sheet. Roast the ribs until the meat starts to pull away from the bones when lifted with tongs, about 1½ hours.

3   While the ribs are roasting, stir together the honey, garlic and orange zest and juice in a small saucepot. Bring to a simmer over medium heat, and cook for 5 minutes, stirring often.

4   After the first 1½ hours of cooking, use a brush to cover the ribs with the glaze every 10 minutes for 30 minutes. The ribs will look really shiny and sticky.

5   Place a medium skillet over medium heat and toast the bread crumbs until they start to brown, about 5 minutes. Add the garlic and sesame seeds, and stir well for 2 minutes, then add the olive oil to coat. Remove from the heat to cool.

CONTINUES

Notes:

+   Make sure you have plenty of napkins and a bowl for the bones—you may want to make a finger bowl of hot water and lemon for each of your guests. This is a nice change from wiping your hands on your pants. The bread crumb mixture is so tasty, I will make extra and use it to jazz up vegetables like cauliflower or green beans.

6   After 2 hours of cooking, the ribs should be tender, and if you lift one end using tongs, they will curl up and break if you apply enough pressure. After adding the last of the glaze, sprinkle the bread crumb mixture in an even layer over the top of the ribs and cook until golden brown and crisp, about 5 minutes more. Remove the ribs from the oven and rest for 5 minutes on the rack before carving between the bones. Arrange on a platter and serve with hot sauce.

Oompahpah Schweinshaxe

Crispy Pork Hocks

'LIVING HIGH OFF THE HOG

2¼ lb (1 kg) fresh pork
hocks

1 medium onion, chopped

1 stalk celery, chopped

1 medium carrot, peeled
and diced

1 Tbsp (15 mL) chopped
fresh thyme leaves

2 Tbsp (30 mL) fancy
molasses

1 cup (250 mL) dark beer

1 tsp (5 mL) cornstarch
(optional)

½ cup (125 mL) diced dill
pickles

Salt and pepper

4 cups (1 L) sauerkraut,
for serving

Crispy Roasted Potatoes
(page 213), for serving

This recipe was inspired by a trip to Bavaria, where our friend Otto did a two-stage cook, first braising to achieve tenderness and then roasting at high heat for the crispy crackling skin. This is ideal for hosting an Oktoberfest party or a craft beer tasting.

---

1   Place the pork hocks in a large saucepot with the onion, celery, carrot and thyme, and add enough water to nearly cover the hocks. Cover the pot and bring to a boil over high heat. Reduce the heat to achieve a gentle simmer and partially cover the pot with the lid. Cook until the hocks are fork-tender, about 1½ hours.

2   Preheat the oven to 375°F (190°C) and line a baking sheet with foil or parchment paper. Set a roasting rack over the baking sheet, and transfer the hocks to the rack. Roast, uncovered, until the skin crisps, blisters and turns a rich brown color, about 1 hour.

3   While the hocks are roasting, return the saucepot to medium-high heat and add the molasses and dark beer. Bring to a boil, uncovered, and then reduce the heat to a full simmer, letting the liquid reduce to 3 cups (750 mL). Using a handheld immersion blender, puree the vegetables into the sauce to thicken (or transfer to a blender to puree), then strain the sauce and return it to the pot. Use a ladle to remove any fat on the surface of the sauce. If it's too thin, dilute the cornstarch in 2 Tbsp (30 mL) of cold water and whisk in; it will thicken as it boils. Stir in the dill pickles and season to taste. Keep warm over low heat.

4   To serve, remove hocks from the oven and let rest for 5 minutes on the rack before splitting. To split, slice lengthwise between the two bones from the thin end down. Serve with the sauce, sauerkraut and roast potatoes.

Notes:

+   The amount of time the pork hocks spend in the hot oven depends on recognizing when the skin is crisp enough— tap on the skin with a spoon, and you should hear a definite brittle noise.

If you want the smoky character of ham, you can use this same method on ham hocks.

Overnight Holiday Ham

The Big Holiday Ham is a staple in our home when we need to feed a crowd without fussing too much—I put a ham on the kitchen island with a bowl of mustard, a knife and some dinner rolls, and our guests know just what to do! If you are hosting an open house, whether during the day or evening, this might just be the recipe to do the trick.

1 (18 lb/8 kg) bone-in smoked ham (hind leg) (see Notes)

GLAZE
½ cup (125 mL) grainy mustard

⅓ cup (80 mL) pure maple syrup

1   Preheat the oven to 275°F (135°C) and place a rack inside a roasting pan.

2   Using a box cutter or sharp paring knife, score the skin in a crisscross pattern (or the fat, if the skin has been removed) every ½ inch (1 cm). This will allow the fat to render and the skin to become crisp. Place the ham in the prepared roasting pan to allow the juices to drain and prevent a hard crust from forming on the bottom. Add 2 cups (500 mL) of water to keep the ham moist during cooking. Roast, uncovered, until the internal temperature reaches 150°F (65°C), for 6 to 8 hours. You can start overnight for a daytime party, or start in the morning for an evening affair.

3   While the ham is cooking, stir together the mustard and maple syrup. Remove the ham from the oven and brush the surface of the ham with half of the glaze. Return the ham to the oven to set the glaze; cook until the internal temperature is 160°F (71°C), about 30 minutes more.

4   Remove the ham from the oven and transfer it to a cutting board to rest for 10 minutes before carving. To carve, use a knife with a long thin blade to cut thin slices across the grain of the meat. You can start at the end opposite the bone and slice into pieces as wide as your palm. Slice enough to get everyone started, then cut as you need for second helpings.

5   Serve with rolls, the remaining mustard glaze, other mustards, pickles, relish or whatever you like.

CONTINUES

Notes

+ I like to go to our local independent butcher to get their ham just 1 or 2 days out of the smokehouse. I choose the kind called "bone-in, skin-on smoked ham." In other words, this is the entire hind leg of a pig that has been brined and then smoked, but still needs to be cooked before eating. Yes, you can buy a fully cooked ham and alter the recipe to reduce the cooking time, but the one I get is the old-school, real deal that takes all day to cook. And it fills the house with the unmistakable aroma of ham, glorious ham! Buying a ham with the bone in gives you the satisfaction that it has been messed with as little as possible. Do not buy a ham that is impossibly square or football-shaped—those are sad hams. Make a little effort to find the right ham, and you will be a happy host.

+ The ham in this photo is a bit of a beast—22 lb (10 kg)—so it would feed at least 30 guests at an open house when served with rolls and some side dishes. Plus, you get the added bonus after the guests leave, in the form of:

1 Bones for soup
2 Slices for sandwiches
3 Julienned pieces for salads, omelets or pasta
4 Diced bits for 1,000 different uses
5 Candles made from the rendered fat put in a jar with a butcher's twine wick (try it, it works!)

+ For hams of different sizes: Preheat the oven to 350°F (180°C). For a smoked, partially cooked ham, cook for around 20 minutes/lb (44 minutes/kg). If the ham is fully cooked, reheat for around 10 minutes/lb (22 minutes/kg).

+ Cooked ham will keep in the fridge for 4 days or in the freezer for up to 3 months.

+ To make stock, combine the bone and any leftover drippings with enough cold water to cover, 2 diced onions, 1 large carrot and 1 stalk of celery. Bring to a boil, skim the surface to remove extra fat, then reduce to a simmer for 1 hour. Strain and store for up to 4 days in the fridge or 3 months in the freezer.

Whole Roast Beast: Lechón

I never used to be a fan of whole roast pig, because it seemed that some parts (the loin) would be overcooked and dry, while others (the shoulder or leg) would not be cooked enough and be tough. Then I visited the Philippines, where they cook a whole small pig for every big occasion: weddings, birthdays, Christmas, New Year's, you name it. They treasure the crisp skin the way the French look at foie gras or Italians see white truffles. I am newly converted to this method of cooking whole pigs, and this is an especially festive way to host a party. The golden, crispy skin covers a juicy, tender and delicately flavored meat that pulls apart. Have plenty of lemons, hot sauce and other condiments on hand so everyone can dress their own "pig-out platter."

___

1   Lay the pig on a large work surface (I do so on top of the plastic wrap it comes in) and wipe with a clean, damp towel soaked in the white vinegar. Remove any remaining bristles from the skin and blood spots inside the belly cavity. Rub 2 Tbsp (30 mL) of the salt into the skin with your hands.

2   Season the cavity with the remaining 1 Tbsp (15 mL) salt and stuff with the green onions, thyme, garlic, lemongrass, lemons and limes. Use a large needle and butcher's twine to sew up the cavity (I use a clean pair of needle-nose pliers to assist if the needle needs help getting through the skin).

3   Preheat a pellet grill to 275°F (135°C) and set the pig in, cavity down. Brush the whole outside with the vegetable oil, then cook for 4 to 5 hours (the timing will vary based on the weight of the pig and the grill that it cooks in). The skin will not be crispy at this point, but the temperature of the leg will climb to 160°F (71°C). You can also do this in an oven or gas grill, but make sure to use a tray to collect the drippings.

20 lb (9 kg) whole pig (order from your butcher 1 week ahead)

½ cup (125 mL) white vinegar

3 Tbsp (45 mL) fine salt, divided

4 bunches green onions, roughly chopped

1 bunch fresh thyme

6 cloves garlic

3 stalks lemongrass, bruised with the back of a knife

4 lemons, sliced into 8 wedges

6 limes, sliced into 6 wedges

¼ cup (60 mL) vegetable oil

Coleslaw (page 257), corn and grilled vegetables, for serving

CONTINUES

4 Increase the temperature to 425°F (218°C) to get color on the skin and make it crisp. This will take 45 minutes, and the final temperature of the shoulder or densest part of the leg should be 170°F (77°C).

5 Remove the pig to a cutting board set over a large tray (to catch any extra drippings) to rest for 10 minutes and allow for the many photos that are sure to be taken. The best way to enjoy this is to have guests help themselves by using a knife, tongs, fork and their hands, but you can also carve it by removing the skin in chunks and cutting it into bite-sized pieces, then also cutting out slices from the larger muscles. Serve with coleslaw and other vegetables of your choosing.

Notes:

+ You can use this method with a pig that weighs up to 40 lb (18 kg), but anything heavier usually requires a larger pig roaster or spit.

+ If you do not get the desired color or crisp on the skin, you can use an electric charcoal lighter or heat gun to blister it and create crackling. I don't recommend a propane torch, as it leaves a bitter taste on the food.

Acknowledgments

Many people contributed to this book and I want to express my appreciation for their efforts.

The photo team: Janis Nicolay and Catherine Therrien were a joy to work with, and recipe testers Lisa Rollo and Amy Pelley helped tighten up recipes when needed.

Robert McCullough at Appetite by Random House has been like family since we met in 1999. He is the calm, gentle voice of publishing and is committed to sharing food knowledge from chef-author to reader. Zoe Maslow was in charge of editing and was often my road map, keeping the project moving ahead in the right direction. She laughed at my corny jokes and made sure that the recipes and notes were easy to follow. I never want to have to play Scrabble against her and copyeditor Lisa Fielding. Designer Jen Griffiths was able to blend the manuscript, artwork and photos together into this beautiful package.

Gary Taxali brought his talent and wit to the pages and we laughed like brats as we planned out the many porcine characters that you've seen. He listened to me as I described the book and created images that are funny and odd and somehow familiar, like a wacky childhood memory. He really got me. I am a long-time fan of Gary's work and owe a thanks to our friend Bob Blumer for introducing us.

Stacey Ash of Ontario Pork and Darcy Fitzgerald of Alberta Pork provided valuable input and helped make the magic happen with Janis's photos.

Le Creuset Canada provided some of the cookware and I thank Raffi and Bianca for this. I've always had a soft spot for the pots, as my mom used a set when I was growing up.

The Sorrenti families at Niagara Sausage cut most of the meat used in the recipe testing and in the photos. They are the nicest, hardest-working,

most salt-of-the-earth people you could meet and they were a big inspiration for writing this book. Thank you Mike, Valerio, Laura and Chris. I once asked Mike to create a particular style of bacon for me; a British style with the loin and belly attached. When I went to pick it up, there was a woman working the counter who didn't know me. After I asked for the bacon, she replied, "Well, you know, I saw that in the cooler and wanted to buy some for myself but Mike said it was for someone special! Who are you? The Chosen One?" I didn't quite know how to respond, so I paused, then said in a booming voice, "Why, yes, as a matter of fact, I *am* the Chosen One!" I told Anna all about this and we laughed, but she still refuses to call me by that name.

Hommer Van der Meer has been my teacher for all questions around meat—this man can trace his family history's connection to butchery back to the 1600s. I've never met anyone who knows more about the meat industry. I call my visits with him "the University of Hommer."

Mika, thanks for the pep talks. I used to think parenting was about dad keeping the daughter positive, but you are so great at inspiring me and getting me excited about work.

And Anna, my wife. She is my biggest fan and most honest critic. She helped me so much with the manuscript, food styling, schedules and everything in between. Anna is graceful and has a delicate beauty but she is the strongest, toughest person I have ever known. She's saved my life and makes me feel so loved every day. I just think the world of her.

And I want to thank you for reading. I wish you many delicious meals, especially with family and friends, because good things start at the dinner table.

Index